Conscious Conversations for Committed Couples

Valerie Monteiro

Contents

Foreword

Life in today's world, where so much competes for our time and attention, relationships often find themselves fighting for space in our crowded lives. Yet, if there's one thing that Valerie's work reminds us of, it's that the quality of our relationships is deeply connected to the quality of our conversations. Over the past 12 years, I've had the privilege of working alongside Valerie, witnessing her deep passion for helping couples not just survive but thrive through intentional, conscious dialogue.

"Conscious Conversations for Committed Couples" is an invitation to engage deliberately in the art of communication. Valerie has dedicated her life's work to exploring how couples can cultivate relationships that are not merely built on shared routines but are profoundly connected through mutual understanding and openness. This book challenges us to consider that true intimacy is not found in grand gestures but in the small, everyday exchanges that deepen our connection over time.

What makes this book unique is its insistence that conscious conversations are necessary at every stage of a relationship. The idea that we should continuously renew our commitment to one another through dialogue is a powerful one. Relationships, like individuals, evolve. The questions we ask and the topics we discuss must evolve alongside us. Valerie's insight is that by regularly engaging in these conversations, couples can anticipate and adapt to change, fostering a resilient bond that can weather life's inevitable storms.

From my perspective as a counsellor, I see immense value in this approach. Too often, couples wait until challenges arise before they address important topics. Valerie's work, however, emphasizes the importance of proactive communication—of not just talking about what is, but also about what could be. It's about setting the stage for a relationship that grows with intention. By creating a space where partners feel seen, heard, and valued, these conscious conversations become a vital practice that sustains connection and strengthens resilience.

Moreover, this book also speaks to a profound spiritual truth: that relationships reflect our inner lives. When we engage in meaningful dialogue with our partners, we also engage with ourselves. Each conversation is an opportunity for self-discovery and growth. Valerie's book beautifully captures this interplay, inviting couples to look inward as they communicate outwardly, fostering both personal and relational transformation.

As I reflect on my journey alongside Valerie, I am reminded of the countless lives she has touched with her wisdom and compassion. This book is a testament to her commitment to helping couples find deeper purpose and connection. It is a guide for those who wish to build relationships that are not only lasting but truly fulfilling. I have no doubt that readers will find in these pages a roadmap to a richer, more meaningful partnership—one conversation at a time.

Derek Boylen

Course Co-ordinator, Couple and Family Therapy, The University of Notre Dame Australia

Director, Centre for Life, Marriage and Family.

ADDRESS TO MY READERS

Dear Readers,

Thank you for choosing this book. By seeking personal growth not only in your relationship but also in every other relationship, you have embarked on a meaningful journey.

Communication is like oxygen; it can either give life or take it away. Your words can be as sweet as honey, or they can sting like bees and cause pain. Choose your words carefully and strive to construct rather than destroy.

When engaging in dialogues, remember that communication extends beyond words. In fact, only 7 percent of our communication is verbal. A significant 38 percent comes from tone, tonality, and gestures, while 55 percent is conveyed through body language. To become an expert in people skills, listen not just with your ears, but with your eyes, heart, and intent.

This book serves as a compass for those seeking guidance, inspiration, and clarity in their journey. Throughout these pages, we delve into the essence of meaningful conversations, reflections, and harmonious practices that enrich our lives. From the tender moments we share when we fall in love, bring a newborn into the world, encourage, and empower our children to be the best version of themselves, to holding the hand of someone passing away, communication is at the heart of our human experience.

Let us start a mission to give life through our words. When wishing someone a happy birthday, make it count. When praising someone in public, let your cheer reach their heart. In moments of sorrow, sometimes silence speaks louder than words; just being there makes a difference.

At the heart of this book is the understanding that we are not alone in our struggles. By engaging in open dialogues, reflecting on our experiences, and embracing our full humanity, we find the strength to overcome challenges and grow. This journey is not just about personal transformation but also about deepening our connections with others and fostering a sense of community and belonging.

Introducing the **SELECT** formula, a method to enhance your conversations and interactions:

- **Still your mind**: Prepare yourself by quieting your thoughts and becoming fully present. This mental stillness allows you to be fully receptive to what the other person is going to talk about.

- **Engage and visualize**: Actively listen and engage with the speaker's words, visualizing their sentences and emotions. This helps you to understand their perspective and context.

- **Look for Empathy**: Delve into your heart to find empathy. Try to see the entire situation from the other person's viewpoint, fostering a deeper connection and understanding.

- **Express and validate**: Communicate your understanding and validate the speaker's pain points. Show them that their feelings are recognized and respected.

- **Compassion, Curiosity, and Clarity**: Seek to show compassion, be curious about their story, and clarify if you understand them correctly. It is important to set aside judgments and focus on them.

- **Timely conversations**: Engage in these heartfelt conversations promptly. Addressing issues in a timely manner can turn situations around and strengthen the bonds between individuals involved.

When reading this book, remember that all recommended conversations are heartfelt. Readers are encouraged to listen intently and with empathy, validate the initiator with the intention to bring resolution. These principles ensure that communication is not only effective but also deeply enriching and transformative.

In a world that often feels fragmented and fast-paced, this book invites you to pause, reflect, and engage in conversations that matter. It is a testament to the resilience of the human spirit and a guide to living a life of authenticity, compassion, and spiritual fulfillment.

May these pages inspire you to embark on a journey of self-discovery, healing, and connection. As you turn to each page, you may find the wisdom and courage to navigate your path with a heart full of love and a spirit attuned to the divine.

Yours truly,

Valerie Monteiro

Module 1
"Pre-Dating Dialogues and Courtship Chats"

Chapter 1

"Know Thyself: The Journey Within

This chapter aims to inspire and guide you as you embark on the journey of dating with intention and clarity. By understanding your values and envisioning your ideal partner, you are laying the groundwork for a conscious and committed relationship.

"Your relationship with yourself sets the tone for every other relationship you have" – *Robert Holden*

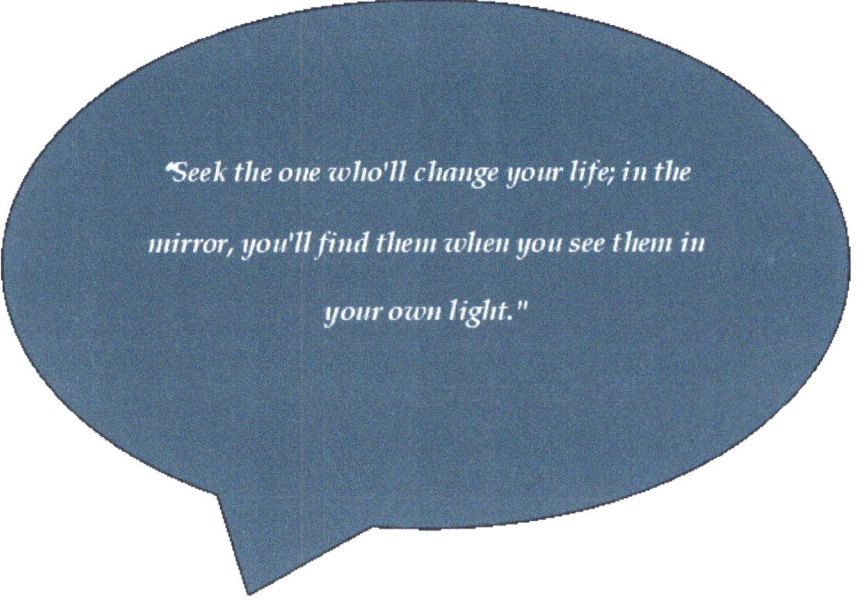

"Seek the one who'll change your life; in the mirror, you'll find them when you see them in your own light."

Introduction

Embarking on the journey of dating with the intention of finding a life partner is both exciting and profound. It is a time filled with possibilities, self-discovery, and the promise of a shared future. Before diving into conversations with potential partners, it is essential to have a heartfelt conversation with yourself. Understanding your values and the kind of person you wish to marry lays a sturdy foundation for a committed and fulfilling relationship. I remember doing this an extraordinarily long time ago and how passionately this topic was discussed with my girlfriends, giggling and yet quite serious about who and where we were going to land up with.

Reflecting on Nuzzi's Journey to Self-Discovery

Nuzzi realized that understanding her values was crucial for her personal growth and finding a compatible partner. She identified core values like honesty, integrity, compassion, loyalty, growth, and adventure. Reflecting on significant moments, she understood how these values shaped her actions, such as standing up for a colleague due to her integrity.

Prioritizing her values, Nuzzi recognized those who were non-negotiable, and which were flexible. This clarity helped her understand what she needed in a partner. Reflecting on past relationships, she saw how mismatched values, like her partner's lack of ambition clashing with her value of growth, led to frustration. Aware of the influence of caregivers, Nuzzi understood that many people struggle to know themselves due to parental expectations. Through self-reflection, she separated her own values from those imposed by her parents, gaining confidence and clarity.

Conversation: Nuzzi and Her Friend on Values

Nuzzi: "I've been doing a lot of self-reflection lately, trying to understand my core values. It's been eye-opening."

Susan: "That sounds profound, Nuzzi. What have you discovered so far?"

Nuzzi: "I realized that honesty, integrity, and compassion are non-negotiable for me. I need a partner who shares these values."

Susan: "That's great insight. How did you come to these conclusions?"

Nuzzi: "I thought about moments in my life when I felt truly aligned with my values, like standing up for a colleague at work. It showed me how important integrity is to me."

Susan: "And what about your past relationships? Did reflecting on them help?"

Nuzzi: "Absolutely. I saw how mismatched values, like my ex's lack of ambition, led to frustration. It helped me understand what I need and want in a partner."

Susan: "It's amazing how self-reflection can bring such clarity. I'm proud of you, Nuzzi."

Nuzzi: "Thanks. It's a continuous journey, but I feel more confident and purposeful now."

They smiled, knowing that Nuzzi's newfound clarity would guide her towards a more fulfilling future.

Your Values

Values are the guiding principles that shape our decisions, behaviors, and interactions. They are the core beliefs that define what is important to us. Taking the time to reflect on your values is a crucial step in understanding yourself and what you seek in a partner.

1. **Identify Your Core Values:** Begin by listing the values that resonate most with you. These include honesty, integrity, compassion, loyalty, growth, and adventure. Think about moments in your life when you felt truly aligned with your values and how they influenced your actions.

2. **Prioritize Your Values:** Not all values hold the same weight. Prioritize them to understand which ones non-negotiable and which ones are flexible. This clarity will help you recognize a compatible partner who shares or respects your core values.

3. **Reflect on Past Relationships:** Consider your past relationships and what worked or did not work. Reflect on how your values played a role in those dynamics. This reflection can provide valuable insights into what you need and want in a future partner.

Envisioning Your Ideal Partner

Once you have a clear understanding of your values, it is time to envision the kind of person you wish to marry. This is not about creating a checklist of superficial traits but rather understanding the deeper qualities that will complement your values and lifestyle.

Character and Integrity: Think about the character traits that are important to you. Do you value kindness, honesty, and a strong moral compass? Consider how these traits will impact your relationship and your ability to trust and rely on each other.

Shared Interests and Goals: While it is not necessary to have all the same interests, having a few shared passions and goals can strengthen your bond. Think about the activities you enjoy and the future you envision. How do you see your partner fitting into this picture?

Emotional Compatibility: Emotional compatibility is key to a healthy relationship. Reflect on how you manage emotions and what you need from a partner in terms of emotional support and communication. Consider how your partner's emotional style will align with yours.

Growth and Development: A fulfilling relationship involves mutual growth. Envision a partner who is committed to personal development and is supportive of your growth journey. Think about how you can inspire and challenge each other to become the best versions of yourselves.

Challenges Young People Face in Finding the Right Partner

Several young people today find it challenging to meet the right person.

For instance, **Sarah, a 28-year-old** marketing professional, has been single for a while. Despite being active on dating apps and attending social events, she struggles to find someone who shares her values and long-term goals. Sarah often feels disheartened by the superficial nature of online dating and the difficulty in finding genuine connections. She is genuinely a lovely human being, pure-hearted, dedicated to work, honest, has great values, and wants a partner, just like her younger siblings found theirs. She wants a family person who is kind and loving because she is kind, honest, and caring. She had to grow quickly when her parents split up, and she carried some of the burden herself with her mom. She found it hard to be with flaky and insincere people who flee when there is a calamity. She completed a self-assessment, changed her profile, and in 3 months, is dating an avid and enthused true love seeker who wants a family, shares her religious beliefs, and is seeking someone as solid, devout, and caring like her.

Similarly, **Vish, 35**, waited until he found a girl who wanted to be a stay-at-home wife and mom, simply because he came from a family of Hindu priests who traditionally wanted their women to stay at home and nurture the family and relationships and that value was of prime importance to him. It was a long wait as he needed it to be the girl's choice as well and did not wish to impose. Once he finally found a girl who vocalized his beliefs and values, he got engaged and married within a few months and is today the proud father of two children living in harmonious family conditions.

Hans, 28, is currently facing his father's wrath. His father is typically very traditional and believes that his one and only son needs to resign from his job and go back to China to live there and support them. Han has fallen in love with an Indonesian girl in Australia, where he works, and is very conflicted about choosing between living his life without the love of his life. Sarawak 25 cannot reconcile to settling down in China and giving up her citizenship in Australia. I have advised Hans to know his core beliefs and understand what is important to him. Core beliefs and values we uphold go a long way in helping us choose what is the most important thing in life and without what we cannot live.

These examples highlight the complexities of modern dating. Young people face numerous challenges, such as balancing career aspirations with personal life, navigating the digital dating landscape, and finding someone who aligns with their values and vision for the future. Despite these difficulties, having a clear understanding of your values and the kind of person you wish to marry can guide you in making more informed and conscious choices in your dating journey.

Activity: Discovering Your Values and True Self

Embarking on the journey to find your values and true self is a rewarding and enlightening process. This activity is designed to help you reflect on what truly matters to you and gain a deeper understanding of your core beliefs and aspirations. Learning about self means learning about your ethnicity, country, up-bringing, personality, social constraints, mental health, economic standing, relationships and so much more.

Step 1: Reflective Journaling

1. **Set the Scene:** Find a quiet and comfortable space where you can reflect without distractions. Have a journal or a piece of paper and a pen ready.

2. **Prompt Questions:** Write down and answer the following questions in your journal:

    o What are the three most important values in my life? Why are they important to me?

    o Think about a time when I felt genuinely happy and fulfilled. What values were being honoured at that moment?

    o What qualities do I admire most in others? How do these qualities reflect my own values?

    o What are my non-negotiables in a relationship? Why are these important to me?

3. **Daily Reflection:** Spend 10-15 minutes each day for a week reflecting on these questions. Allow yourself to write freely and honestly.

Step 2: Values Clarification Exercise

1. **Create a Values List:** Write down a list of values that resonate with you. Here are some examples to get you started: honesty, integrity, compassion, loyalty, growth, adventure, creativity, family, health, spirituality, and community.

2. **Prioritize Your Values:** Once you have your list, prioritize them by placing them in order of importance. Identify your top five core values.

3. **Reflect on Your Top Values:** For each of your top five values, write a short paragraph about why this value is important to you and how it influences your life decisions and actions.

Step 3: Vision Board Creation

1. **Gather Materials:** Collect magazines, newspapers, scissors, glue, and a large piece of paper or a poster board.

2. **Visualize Your Values:** Cut out images, words, and phrases that represent your top values and the kind of person you wish to become. Arrange them on your poster board to create a vision board.

3. **Display Your Vision Board:** Place your vision board somewhere you can see it daily. Let it serve as a visual reminder of your values and the person you aspire to be.

Step 4: Self-Reflection and Sharing

1. **Self-Reflection:** Take some time to reflect on what you have learned about yourself through this activity. Consider how your values align with your current life and relationships.

2. **Share with a Trusted Friend or Mentor:** Discuss your reflections and vision board with a trusted friend or mentor. Sharing your insights can provide additional clarity and support.

Conclusion

This activity is a powerful starting point for discovering your values and true self. By engaging in reflective journaling, clarifying your values, creating a vision board, and sharing your insights, you will gain a deeper understanding of what truly matters to you. This self-awareness will guide you in making conscious and intentional choices in your dating journey and beyond.

Having a conversation with yourself about your values and the kind of person you wish to marry is a powerful step towards finding a committed and loving partner. It sets the stage for conscious dating, where you are clear about what you seek and what you bring to a relationship. Remember, this journey is as much about self-discovery as it is about finding the right partner. Embrace this process with an open heart and mind, and trust that the right person will align with your values and vision for the future.

References

Robitschek, C., & Thoen, M. A. (2015). Personal growth and development. In J. C. Wade, L. I. Marks, & R. D. Hetzel (Eds.), Positive psychology on the college campus (pp. 219-238). Oxford University Press.

Bauer, J. J. (2021). The transformative self: Personal growth, narrative identity, and a good life. Oxford University Press. https://doi.org/10.1093/oso/9780199970742.001.0001

Moustakas, C. E. (Ed.). (1956). The self; explorations in personal growth. Harper.

Amato, P. R. (2010). The changing context of family: Family structure, diversity, and the future of family theory. Journal of Marriage and Family, 72(3), 659-674.

Coontz, S. (2005). Marriage, a history: From obedience to intimacy, or how love conquered marriage. Viking.

Chapter 2

Before We Became Us: A Glimpse into Your Partner's Past

This chapter aims to inspire and guide you as you explore each other's past and the values that have shaped who you are today. By engaging in these meaningful conversations, you are laying the groundwork for a conscious and committed relationship.

"Family is where we become who we are, shaped by the love and values that we are given."

By knowing your partner's childhood tales and family ties,

Their deepest wounds and the roots of their cries,

You forge a bridge to their past so profound,

Strengthening your bond, feeling their pain's sound,

Especially in conflicts, where empathy is found."

Introduction

As you embark on the journey towards a committed relationship, understanding your partner's life before they meet you is crucial. This chapter focuses on the importance of exploring each other's family of origin, past experiences, and the values that have shaped who you are today. These conversations can deepen your connection and provide a solid foundation for your future together.

Understanding Family of Origin

Your family of origin plays a significant role in shaping your beliefs, behaviours, and expectations in relationships. By discussing your family backgrounds, you can gain insights into each other's upbringing and how it influences your current relationship dynamics.

1. **Sharing Family Stories:** Take turns sharing stories about your childhood, family traditions, and momentous events. This can help you understand the context in which your partner grew up and the values that were instilled in them.

2. **Discussing Family Roles:** Talk about the roles each family member played in your lives. Understanding these roles can provide insights into your partner's expectations and behaviours in your relationship. For example, if your partner was the caregiver in their family, they might naturally take on a nurturing role in your relationship.

3. **Exploring Family Dynamics:** Discuss the dynamics within your families, such as how conflicts were managed, how affection was expressed, and how decisions were made. This can help you understand your partner's communication style and approach to conflict resolution.

Understanding behaviours from dysfunctional families for a better insight into your partner's ways and habits.

Sharing Family Stories

Meet Dymphna and Nestor, a couple who recently decided to dive deeper into their relationship by exploring their family backgrounds. They took turns sharing stories about their childhood, family traditions, and noteworthy events. Dymphna recounted her annual summer trips with her family to the beach, a tradition that instilled in her a love for the ocean and a sense of adventure. Nestor shared memories of his family's Sunday dinners, which were filled with laughter, debates, and delicious food, highlighting the importance of family bonding and open communication.

Discussing Family Roles

As they delved into their family roles, Dymphna revealed that she was the eldest sibling and often took on a caregiving role for her younger siblings. This nurturing behaviour naturally extended into her relationship with Nestor. Nestor, on the other hand, was the mediator in his family, often stepping in to resolve conflicts between his parents and siblings. Understanding these roles provided insights into their behaviours and expectations in their relationship.

Exploring Family Dynamics

Dymphna and Nestor discussed the dynamics within their families, such as how conflicts were overseen and how affection was expressed. Dymphna's family tended to avoid conflicts, sweeping issues under the rug, while Nestor's family encouraged open discussions to resolve disagreements. This exploration helped them understand their differing communication styles and approach to conflict resolution, paving the way for more effective interactions.

Understanding Behaviours from Dysfunctional Families

Cassie and Ronnie also examined how growing up in dysfunctional families influenced their behaviours and habits.

Control

Cassie grew up in a controlled environment where expressing her feelings was often discouraged. She shared, "I find it hard to share my feelings." Ronnie responded empathetically, "I understand that sharing can be difficult, especially if you were always controlled. Take your time and know that this is a safe space for your feelings."

Perfectionism

In Ronnie's family, the expectation of perfection was high, and he often felt like nothing he did was ever good enough. He confessed, "I feel like nothing I do is ever good enough." Cassie reassured him, "Perfection can be exhausting. It is okay to have flaws and imperfections. You are enough just as you are."

Blame

Ronnie realized that a culture of blaming others was deeply ingrained in his family. During conflicts, he would often deflect responsibility. "It's not my fault; you always make things difficult," he admitted. Cassie gently pointed out, "Blaming others might have been a coping mechanism in the past. Let's work together to find constructive ways to address our issues."

Denial of 5 Freedoms

Cassie struggled with asserting her personal needs and desires, feeling that her thoughts did not matter. "I don't feel like my thoughts matter," she shared. Ronnie responded, "Your thoughts and feelings are important. You have every right to express them here."

No Talk Rule

In Cassie's family, open communication was discouraged, and she was taught to keep her opinions to herself. "I was taught to keep my opinions to myself," she said. Ronnie reassured her, "It's okay to share your opinions with me. Your voice deserves to be heard."

Myth Making

Ronnie often minimized his problems by comparing them to others' worse experiences, invalidating his genuine feelings. "This isn't as bad as what others go through," he would say. Cassie emphasized, "Your experiences and feelings are valid, regardless of what others may face. Let's address them together."

Incompletion

Cassie noticed that conflicts in her family were often left unresolved, leading to lingering frustration. "Things never seemed to get resolved in my family," she remarked. Ronnie agreed, "It's important to find a resolution. Let's work through our issues until we both feel at peace."

Unreliability

Growing up with unreliable caregivers, Ronnie developed trust issues. "I have a hard time trusting people," he confessed. Cassie offered her support, "Trust can be difficult to build, especially if you've been let down before. I'm here to build that trust with you, step by step."

Through these heartfelt discussions, Ronnie and Cassie gained valuable insights into each other's upbringing and how it influenced their current relationship dynamics. By understanding and addressing these deeply ingrained behaviours, they strengthened their bond and built a more supportive and loving partnership.

Similar values and customs, dissimilar upbringing can cause huge rifts.

Bryce and Veronica, both Roman Catholics and neighbours, shared strong family values but had vastly different upbringings. Bryce's strict, controlling parents instilled discipline through punishment and criticism, while Veronica's generous, religious parents emphasized helping others but imposed strict rules.

After marriage, Bryce's need for control clashed with Veronica's desire for community and generosity. Bryce, scarred by his father's mistrust due to being cheated, imposed restrictions on Veronica, who felt bullied and stifled. Despite her regular prayers, Veronica struggled to cope with Bryce's controlling nature.

Their marriage suffered until they sought help and understood the impact of their family origins. Through counselling, they learned to respect each other's backgrounds, encouraging individual freedom and addressing unhealthy behaviours. This understanding allowed them to build a harmonious life together, honouring both their family values.

Healing Conversation: Bryce and Veronica

After several weeks of counselling, Bryce and Veronica sat down for a heart-to-heart conversation. They chose a quiet evening at home, ensuring there would be no distractions.

Bryce: "Veronica, I want to start by saying how grateful I am that we've been working through this together. I know I've been controlling and that it has hurt you deeply. I'm truly sorry for that."

Veronica: (nodding) "I appreciate your honesty, Bryce. It has been difficult for me to express how stifled I've felt. I grew up in a home were helping others and being open was encouraged and feeling like I couldn't do that here has been really hard."

Bryce: "I see that now. My upbringing made me fear losing control and being hurt, but I understand that this fear has caused me to impose too many restrictions on you. I don't want to be like that anymore."

Veronica: "It is reassuring to hear that. I want us to create a home where we can both be ourselves and support each other. I need to be able to help others and feel like I can make my own choices."

Bryce: "I want that too. From now on, I will work on trusting more and letting go of the need to control everything. I will support you in the ways that matter to you, including your desire to help others."

Veronica: "Thank you, Bryce. And I promise to communicate my feelings and needs more openly, instead of letting them build up inside. I want us to be partners in every sense."

Bryce: "Absolutely. Let's make a pact to check in with each other regularly, to talk about our feelings and any issues that come up. I believe we can build a stronger relationship by being open and supportive."

Veronica: "Agreed. I'm hopeful for our future, Bryce. I believe we can overcome this together and create a loving, respectful home."

They sealed their conversation with a hug, both feeling a renewed sense of hope and commitment to their relationship. They knew it wouldn't be easy, but they were determined to work through their issues with love and understanding.

A Tale of Compromise and Understanding

Leona and Scott, both headstrong and ambitious, came from vastly different backgrounds. Scott, influenced by English and Scottish military traditions, valued discipline, duty, and solitude. In contrast, Leona's family was lively, enjoying parties, entertainment, and a strong sense of community.

Scott preferred small, reserved gatherings, while Leona loved large, joyous celebrations. Their family origins significantly shaped their preferences and values. Scott's upbringing emphasized structure and simplicity, whereas Leona's background celebrated social connections and exuberance.

As they navigated their relationship, they recognized the need to balance their differing values. Scott learned to appreciate the warmth and joy of Leona's family gatherings, while Leona embraced the simplicity and tranquillity that Scott valued. Through compromise and adjustment, they found solutions to their arguments, creating a unique blend of traditions that honoured both their backgrounds.

In the end, their love and understanding allowed them to build a harmonious life together, blending their diverse family origins and creating new traditions of their own.

Healing Conversation: Leona and Scott

It was a quiet Sunday afternoon when Leona and Scott decided to sit down for a heartfelt conversation. They chose their cozy living room, filled with mementos from both their families, symbolizing the blend of their lives together.

Leona: (smiling warmly) "Scott, I'm really glad we're taking the time to talk about this. I know our backgrounds are so different, and sometimes it feels like we're from different worlds."

Scott: (nodding) "Absolutely, Leona. I've been thinking a lot about how our upbringings have shaped us. Growing up, discipline and order were everything to my family. I realize now that it made me appreciate structure and simplicity."

Leona: "And for me, my family was all about social connections and big gatherings. I grew up with so much noise, laughter, and music. It was a different kind of joy."

Scott: "I see that now. At first, I didn't understand why you wanted such large celebrations, but I see how much they mean to you. I'm sorry if my need for solitude made you feel isolated."

Leona: "Thank you, Scott. I appreciate that. I also understand your need for calm and order. It's something I've learned to value. But I've felt stifled at times, like I couldn't be myself."

Scott: "I don't want you to feel that way. I want us to find a balance where we both feel comfortable. Let's try to incorporate more of each other's values. I can learn to enjoy the bigger gatherings, and you can find peace in our quieter moments."

Leona: (smiling) "I think that sounds wonderful. Maybe we can plan our gatherings together, ensuring they have both the joy of my family's traditions and the simplicity you cherish."

Scott: "I like that idea. It's important to me that we respect each other's backgrounds and create new traditions that are uniquely ours."

Leona: "Agreed. Compromise and understanding have gotten us this far, and I believe it will continue to strengthen our bond."

Scott: "Leona, I love you deeply, and I'm committed to making this work. Let's keep communicating openly and respecting our differences."

Leona: "I love you too, Scott. Let's make our life together a beautiful blend of both our worlds."

They hugged, feeling a renewed sense of connection and commitment. By acknowledging their differences and finding ways to integrate their values, Leona and Scott continued to build a harmonious and fulfilling life together.

Melwyn and Sally:

Sally's family valued independence and self-reliance, while Mel's family emphasized togetherness and mutual support. Through their conversations, Mel and Sally learned to appreciate each other's perspectives and find ways to integrate both values into their relationship.

Healing Conversation: Sally and Mel

One evening, Sally and Mel decided to sit down and have an open conversation about their differing family values. They chose their cozy living room, a space where they both felt comfortable and safe.

Mel: (gently) "Sally, I have been thinking a lot about how different our families are. Your family values independence and self-reliance so much, while mine emphasizes togetherness and mutual support. I think it's important that we talk about how to blend these values in our relationship."

Sally: (nodding) "I agree, Mel. I know that sometimes my need for independence might come across as me not wanting to be close, but that's

14

not true. It's just how I was raised."

Mel: "I understand that. And I want you to know that your independence is one of the things I love about you. At the same time, my family's emphasis on togetherness has taught me the importance of mutual support and being there for each other."

Sally: "I appreciate that, Mel. I think both our values have their strengths. Independence has taught me to be self-reliant, but I also see the beauty in the support and closeness your family shares."

Mel: "Exactly. I believe we can integrate both values into our relationship. We can support each other while also respecting our need for personal space and independence."

Sally: "I think that's a great idea. Maybe we can set aside certain times for us to be together and focus on supporting each other, while also having times where we do our own things and respect each other's space."

Mel: "I love that plan. It is s all about finding a balance. I will make an effort to respect your need for independence, and I hope you can understand my desire for togetherness."

Sally: "Absolutely. Let's communicate openly about our needs and find ways to support each other. I want us to feel connected and strong, no matter how different our backgrounds are."

Mel: "Me too, Sally. I love you, and I believe that by understanding and respecting our differences, we can create a beautiful life together."

Sally: "I love you too, Mel. Let's continue to learn from each other and make our relationship even stronger."

They embraced, feeling a renewed sense of connection and commitment. By appreciating each other's perspectives and integrating their values, Sally and Mel were able to create a harmonious balance in their relationship, honouring both independence and togetherness.

Activity: Family of Origin Exploration

Step 1: Reflective Journaling

1. **Set the Scene:** Find a quiet and comfortable space where you can reflect without distractions. Have a journal or a piece of paper and a pen ready.

2. **Prompt Questions:** Write down and answer the following questions in your journal:

o   What are some of my favourite childhood memories? How did they shape my values and beliefs?

o   What roles did my family members play in my life? How do these roles influence my current relationships?

o   How was conflict managed in my family? How does this impact my approach to conflict in my relationship?

o   What family traditions or values do I want to carry forward into my own family?

Step 2: Partner Discussion

1. **Share Your Reflections:** Take turns sharing your reflections with your partner. Listen actively and empathetically to each other's stories and experiences.

2. **Ask Open-Ended Questions:** Encourage deeper conversation by asking open-ended questions such as:

    o   How did your family celebrate holidays and special occasions?

    o   What was your relationship like with your siblings or extended family?

    o   How did your parents show love and affection?

3. **Discuss Similarities and Differences:** Identify any similarities and differences in your family backgrounds. Discuss how these might influence your relationship and how you can navigate any potential challenges.

Conclusion

Understanding your partner's family of origin and their life before meeting you is a vital step in building a strong and committed relationship. These conversations can help you appreciate each other's backgrounds, recognize the influences that shape your behaviours, and create a shared vision for your future together. Embrace this journey with curiosity and openness, and let these discussions deepen your connection and mutual understanding.

References

Barrett, L. F., & Lane, R. D. (2009). Emotion and consciousness: Integrating cognitive, affective, and biological perspectives. Psychology Press.

Coates, J. (2016). Understanding and managing your emotions: A guide to self-awareness and emotional intelligence. Routledge.

Siegel, J. P. (2020). Digging deeper: An object relations couple therapy update. Family Process, 59(1), 10-20. https://doi.org/10.1111/famp.12509

Zayas, V., Urganci, B., & Strycharz, S. (2024). Out of sight but in mind: Experimentally activating partner representations in daily life buffers against common stressors. Emotion. Advance online publication. https://doi.org/10.1037/emo0001419

Kimmes, J. G., Zheng, Y., Morris, K. L., Marroquin, C. G., Rudaz, M., & Smedley, D. K. (2024). You are not fully present with me: How own and perceived partner mindfulness shape relationship outcomes. Journal of Family Psychology. Advance online publication. https://doi.org/10.1037/fam0001290

Chapter 3

Crafting Our Legacy: Exploring Family Paths Together

This chapter aims to inspire and guide you as you explore each other's expectations about starting a family. By engaging in these meaningful conversations, you are laying the groundwork for a conscious and committed relationship.

"Other things may change us, but we start and end with the family" -

Anthony Brandt

"Family is family, from the start to the end,

The ones you begin with, and those you befriend.

Through life's winding journey, new bonds you may sway,

Each heart you hold dear, family gained on the way.

Introduction

Starting a family or thinking about having kids is one of the most significant decisions a couple can make. It involves not only practical considerations but also emotional and relational aspects. Before getting married, it is essential to have open and honest conversations about each other's expectations regarding starting a family. This chapter will guide you through the types of conversations you need to engage in to ensure that you and your partner are on the same page.

Discussing Family Expectations

Understanding each other's expectations about starting a family can help prevent misunderstandings and conflicts in the future. Here are some key areas to explore:

1. **Desire to Have Children:** Begin by discussing whether both of you want to have children. This might seem like an obvious question, but it is crucial to ensure that you both have similar desires regarding parenthood.

2. **Timing and Readiness:** Talk about when you would like to start a family. Consider factors such as career goals, financial stability, and personal readiness. Understanding each other's timelines can help you plan accordingly.

3. **Parenting Styles and Values:** Discuss your views on parenting and the values you want to instill in your children. Consider how you were raised and what aspects of your upbringing you would like to carry forward or do differently.

4. **Role Expectations:** Talk about the roles each of you expects to play in raising children. This includes discussing responsibilities such as childcare, household chores, and financial contributions.

5. **Support Systems:** Consider the support systems you have in place, such as family, friends, and community resources. Discuss how you will rely on these supports and how they will impact your parenting journey.

Dialogue

Rina and Kailash

Conversation: Rina and Kailash

Rina and Kailash sat down in their living room, the tension between them palpable. They had been through so much together, and it was time to have an honest conversation about their struggles.

Kailash: (gently) "Rina, I know we've been through a lot, and I can see how much pain you're in. I want you to know that I'm here for you, no matter what."

Rina: (tearfully) "Kailash, I want children so much, but my past trauma makes it so hard. I avoid intimacy because I can't get past the pain. It's affecting our marriage, and I feel so guilty."

Kailash: "You don't have to feel guilty. I married you because I love you,

19

and I always will. I thought things would get better over time, but I realize now that we need help to move forward."

Rina: "I appreciate your patience and love. I think it's time we seek professional help. I can't do this alone anymore, and I don't want our marriage to suffer."

Kailash: "I agree. Let's find a therapist who can help us navigate this. It's important for both of us to heal and move forward together."

(After seeking help)

Rina: "Kailash, the therapy has been tough, but I feel like I'm starting to heal. I've been able to confront my past, and it's helping me feel closer to you."

Kailash: "I'm so proud of you, Rina. I can see the progress you're making, and it means the world to me. We're in this together."

Rina: "I feel more hopeful now. With your support and the therapist's guidance, I believe we can overcome this. I want to build a family with you."

Kailash: "And we will, Rina. We'll take it one step at a time. Our love and understanding will see us through."

Several years later, after much healing and effort, Rina and Kailash were blessed with a beautiful daughter. Their journey underscored the importance of addressing deep-seated issues to build a strong, loving future together.

"The greatest healing therapy is friendship and love." – Hubert H. Humphrey

Connie and Sean

Connie and Sean made a mutual decision not to have children. Connie was firm in her belief that she did not want to bring kids into this world, and since this was Sean's second marriage and he already had a child from his previous marriage, it suited him perfectly. They are both happily married and content with their decision.

Their story highlights the importance of clear intentions and mutual agreement before entering marriage. When one partner wants children and the other does not, it can lead to significant challenges and emotional turmoil. Clear communication and shared goals are crucial for a harmonious relationship.

Considering the Unique Experiences of Gay and Lesbian Couples

For gay and lesbian couples, starting a family often involves additional considerations and conversations. These discussions can help ensure that both partners are aligned in their expectations and prepared for the journey ahead.

1. **Family Planning Options:** Discuss the distinct options available for starting a family, such as adoption, surrogacy, sperm or egg donation, and co-parenting arrangements. Understanding each other's preferences and comfort levels with these options is crucial.

2. **Legal Considerations:** Explore the legal aspects of starting a family, including parental rights, adoption laws, and any necessary legal agreements. It is important to be informed about the legal landscape and how it may impact your family planning decisions.

3. **Support Systems:** Consider the support systems available to you, including LGBTQ+ friendly healthcare providers, legal advisors, and community resources. Discuss how you will navigate potential challenges and seek support when needed.

4. **Cultural and Social Factors:** Reflect on how your cultural and social backgrounds may influence your family planning decisions. Discuss any concerns or challenges you may face and how you can support each other through them.

John and Michael: Building a Family and Financial Harmony

John comes from a conservative family that initially struggled with his sexuality. Michael, on the other hand, was raised in a more accepting environment. They both understand the importance of family and have worked hard to build bridges with John's family, fostering a sense of acceptance and love.

Starting a Family: John and Michael have always dreamed of starting a family. After many discussions and research, they decided to adopt. They are now proud parents to a beautiful daughter, Emma, who has brought immense joy and purpose to their lives.

Financial Planning: Both John and Michael are financially savvy. They regularly consult with a financial advisor to ensure they are on track with their savings and investments. They also have a joint account for household expenses and individual accounts for personal spending, which helps maintain financial harmony.

Dialogue: John and Michael

John: "Michael, I have been thinking a lot about starting a family. I know it's something we both want deeply."

Michael: "Absolutely, John. I've always dreamed of us having children. Adoption seems like the best path for us."

John: "I agree. Let's do more research and find an agency that aligns with our values. And we should definitely talk to our financial advisor to make sure we are prepared."

Michael: "Good idea. I think we're in a good place financially, but it is important to make sure we're ready for this new responsibility."

John: "I am excited, Michael. I believe Emma will bring so much joy into our lives."

Michael: "Me too, John. Our family will be complete, and I'm so grateful for the journey we've been on together."

2. Sarah and Emily: A Journey of Love and Parenthood

Sarah and Emily's love story began in college, where they bonded over late-night study sessions and a mutual passion for social justice. Sarah values independence and self-growth, while Emily emphasizes compassion and community. Emily's family has always been supportive of her sexuality, while Sarah faced initial resistance from her parents. Over time, through open conversations and patience, Sarah's parents have come to accept and love Emily as part of their family.

Starting a Family: Sarah and Emily decided to start a family through IVF. They now have twin boys, Liam and Noah, who have brought a new dimension of love and responsibility to their lives. They balance their careers and parenting with the help of a dedicated support network of friends and family.

Dialogue: Sarah and Emily

Sarah: "Emily, I have been thinking a lot about starting a family. I know it is something we have always wanted."

Emily: "Yes, Sarah. Having children has always been part of our dream. I think IVF is the right choice for us."

Sarah: "I agree. Let's reach out to a fertility clinic and get more information on the process. And we should make sure we have the support we need from our friends and family."

Emily: "Absolutely. We are fortunate to have such a strong network. I think Liam and Noah will bring so much joy and love into our lives."

Sarah: "I am so excited for this next chapter, Emily. Our family is growing, and I couldn't be happier."

Emily: "Me too, Sarah. Our love and shared values will guide us through this journey of parenthood."

Activity: Exploring Family Expectations

Step 1: Reflective Journaling

1. **Set the Scene:** Find a quiet and comfortable space where you can reflect without distractions. Have a journal or a piece of paper and a pen ready.

2. **Prompt Questions:** Write down and answer the following questions in your journal:

   o   Do I want to have children? Why or why not?

   o   When do I feel ready to start a family? What factors influence this decision?

   o   What parenting values and styles are important to me?

   o   What roles do I expect to play in raising children?

   o   What support systems do I have in place for starting a family?

Step 2: Partner Discussion

1. **Share Your Reflections:** Take turns sharing your reflections with your partner. Listen actively and empathetically to each other's thoughts and feelings.

2. **Ask Open-Ended Questions:** Encourage deeper conversation by asking open-ended questions such as:

   o   How do you envision our life with children?

   o   What are your biggest hopes and fears about starting a family?

   o   How do you think our families will react to us starting a family? What support systems are available to me as an LGBTQ+ individual or couple?

   o   How do my cultural and social backgrounds influence my family planning decisions?

3. **Discuss Similarities and Differences:** Identify any similarities and differences in your expectations. Discuss how you can navigate any potential challenges and find common ground.

Conclusion

Having conversations about starting a family is a vital step in building a strong and committed relationship. These discussions can help you understand each other's expectations, align your goals, and create a shared vision for your future together. Embrace this journey with openness and honesty, and let these conversations deepen your connection and mutual understanding. These narratives emphasize the importance of open communication and addressing critical issues before marriage to build a durable foundation for the future.

References

Amato, P. R. (2010). The changing context of family: Family structure, diversity, and the future of family theory. Journal of Marriage and Family, 72(3), 659-674.

Coontz, S. (2005). Marriage, a history: From obedience to intimacy, or how love conquered marriage. Viking.

Doherty, W. J., & Beaton, A. (2014). The marriage and family experience: Intimate relationships in a changing society (12th ed.). Pearson.

Kellerman, S. (2010). Intimate relationships (6th ed.). McGraw-Hill.

Popenoe, D. (1993). American family decline, 1960-1990: A review and appraisal. Journal of Marriage and Family, 55(3), 527-555.

Chapter 4

Wedding Wallets: Managing Finances and Budgets Together

This chapter aims to inspire and guide you as you explore each other's financial expectations and plan for your wedding. By engaging in these meaningful conversations, you are laying the groundwork for a conscious and committed relationship.

"Money is a terrible master but an excellent servant." P.T. Barnum

Spoil me with love, I can finance my own,

No gifts, no money, just time alone.

Your attention, your love, that's all I seek,

Care for my soul, my heart, make me weak.

Spoil me with treasures that can't be bought,

For it's your love and care that I've always sought."

Introduction

Planning a wedding is an exciting milestone, but it also comes with significant financial considerations. Before getting married, it's essential to have open and honest conversations about your financial status and how you plan to finance your wedding. This chapter will guide you through the types of conversations you need to engage in to ensure that you and your partner are financially aligned and prepared for this important event.

Discussing Financial Status

Understanding each other's financial situation is crucial for building a sturdy foundation for your marriage. Here are some key areas to explore:

1. **Current Financial Situation:** Begin by discussing your current financial status, including income, savings, debts, and expenses. Transparency in this area is vital for building trust and making informed decisions together.

2. **Financial Goals and Priorities:** Talk about your short-term and long-term financial goals. This includes discussing your priorities, such as buying a home, saving for retirement, or traveling. Understanding each other's financial aspirations can help you align your goals and create a shared vision for your future.

3. **Spending and Saving Habits:** Discuss your spending and saving habits. Are you a spender or a saver? How do you manage your finances? Understanding each other's financial habits can help you develop a budget that works for both of you.

4. **Credit Scores and Reports:** Share your credit scores and reports with each other. This can provide insights into your financial health and help you plan for any necessary improvements.

5. **Gambling addiction or debt/excessive loans:** Gambling addiction and excessive debt are serious issues that can significantly strain a marriage or relationship. These problems are often not discussed openly, but they are critical to address. Many relationships have been damaged or even broken due to one partner accumulating significant debt or struggling with a gambling addiction. It is crucial to be vigilant and have open conversations about these issues before committing to a long-term relationship.

6. **Understanding the Impact:** Gambling addiction can lead to severe financial instability, emotional distress, and a breakdown in trust. The compulsive needs to gamble can result in the depletion of savings, accumulation of debt, and financial secrecy, which erodes the foundation of a relationship12. Similarly, excessive loans and unmanaged debt can create constant stress and conflict, making it difficult for couples to achieve financial stability and harmony.

7. **The Importance of Early Conversations:** Before settling down with a partner, it is essential to discuss financial habits, debts, and any potential issues related to gambling. Understanding each other's financial situation and attitudes towards money can help prevent future conflicts and ensure that both partners are on the same page.

This initiative-taking approach can save a lot of heartache and stress later.

Financing the Wedding

Planning a wedding involves various expenses, and it's important to discuss how you will finance this special day. Here are some key areas to explore:

1. **Budgeting for the Wedding:** Create a detailed budget for your wedding, including all potential expenses such as venue, catering, attire, and decorations. Discuss how much you are willing to spend and how you will allocate your funds.

2. **Saving for the Wedding:** Talk about how you will save for your wedding. This might involve setting up a dedicated savings account, cutting back on non-essential expenses, or finding additional sources of income.

3. **Contributions from Family:** Discuss whether you will receive any financial contributions from family members. If so, clarify the amount and how it will be used. It is important to have clear communication with your families to avoid any misunderstandings.

4. **Managing Wedding Expenses:** Consider how you will manage wedding expenses, such as using credit cards, taking out a loan, or paying in instalments. Discuss the pros and cons of each option and decide what works best for you.

Considering Cultural Traditions: Dowry Expectations

In some cultures, dowry expectations play a significant role in wedding planning. It is important to discuss whether you are willing to participate in these traditions and how they might impact your financial planning.

1. **Middle Eastern Weddings:** In many Middle Eastern cultures, dowry is considered a legal right for women and is mandatory at Islamic weddings. The dowry, often given by the groom to the bride, can include money, jewellery, or other valuable items. Discussing your willingness to participate in this tradition and how it aligns with your values is crucial.

2. **Indian Weddings:** The dowry system in India, despite being outlawed, continues to influence wedding practices2. Dowries can be substantial and may include cash, gold, and household items. It is important to discuss whether you view this tradition as a burden or a meaningful cultural practice and how it will affect your financial planning.

Dialogue

Darryl and Roanna: A Journey of Love and Financial Discipline

Darryl and Roanna, college sweethearts, faced a turning point when Darryl's family moved to Australia. Roanna's conservative parents ensured her future by getting her engaged before the move. Initially, they had a humble wedding due to limited funds. Two years later, after securing stable jobs and saving diligently, they celebrated with a traditional church wedding. Darryl arranged a second ceremony in their hometown, allowing loved ones to join in their joy.

Fifteen years later, they mastered budgeting, taking annual family holidays and, after 14 years of saving, moved into their dream house. By balancing traditions and respecting their parents' wishes, they lived modestly until financially stable. Darryl and Roanna's story exemplifies patience, financial discipline, and mutual respect, honoring their heritage and commitment.

Conversation: Darryl and Roanna

Roanna: "Darryl, remember when we first moved to Australia? It feels like a lifetime ago."

Darryl: (smiling) "I do. It was challenging, but we made it through together. I think our humble beginnings taught us the value of patience and saving."

Roanna: "Absolutely. Having that initial simple wedding and then our traditional ceremony later was a beautiful way to honor both our families and our financial situation."

Darryl: "And look at us now, fifteen years later. We have managed to balance our finances so well that we can take yearly holidays with the kids and finally move into our dream house."

Roanna: "It has not always been easy, but budgeting and respecting each other's values really paid off. I'm so proud of what we have accomplished together."

Darryl: "Me too, Roanna. Our journey proves that with discipline and mutual respect, we can achieve our dreams while staying true to our roots."

Roanna: "Here is to many more years of love, patience, and financial harmony."

They embraced, feeling a deep sense of gratitude and accomplishment. Their story continued to inspire those around them, demonstrating the power of commitment and careful planning.

They embraced, feeling a deep sense of gratitude and accomplishment. Their story continued to inspire those around them, demonstrating the power of commitment and careful planning.

Aisha and Omar: Balancing Tradition with Practicality

Aisha and Omar, from affluent Middle Eastern families, faced the cultural expectation of a dowry. Instead of feeling pressured, they honoured it practically. Their parents gifted them a lavish 3-day wedding celebration. Aisha, valuing practicality, requested her parents contribute to a house deposit instead of traditional gifts, setting a strong financial foundation. Omar's family, embracing a progressive outlook, also contributed to the house deposit, supporting their shared vision. Their story exemplifies balancing cultural traditions with practical decisions, ensuring financial security while honouring their heritage.

Conversation: Aisha and Omar

Aisha: "Omar, I am so grateful our families supported our vision for the future. Asking for contributions towards a house deposit instead of traditional dowry gifts made such a difference."

Omar: "Absolutely, Aisha. It allowed us to start our life on solid ground without feeling burdened by cultural expectations. Plus, the wedding was still a beautiful blend of tradition and modernity."

Aisha: "I agree. Our 3-day celebration was perfect, and we respected our heritage in a meaningful way. I'm glad our families understood and supported our practical approach."

Omar: "Me too. By prioritizing our future, we honoured our roots and set ourselves up for a harmonious and financially secure life together."

Aisha: "Here's to balancing tradition with practicality and creating our own path."

They smiled, feeling proud of their decisions and grateful for their supportive families, ready to build a bright future together.

Example 1: Discussing Budgeting

Scenario: Denzil and Rachel are discussing their monthly budget.

Denzil: "Hey Rach, I was looking at our expenses for this month, and I think we might need to adjust our budget a bit. What do you think?"

Rachel: "Sure, Denzil I noticed we spent a bit more on dining out. We can try cooking at home more often?"

Denzil: "That is a great idea! We can also look for some new recipes to try together. How about we set a limit for dining out and allocate more for groceries?"

Rachel: "I love that plan. Let us also set aside some money for a fun date night once a month. It will be a nice treat!"

Reflection: This conversation shows how John and Emily approach budgeting as a team, suggesting solutions and making compromises to achieve their financial goals.

Example 2: Planning for a Major Purchase

Scenario: Ratna and Ajit are planning to buy a new car.

Ratna: "Ajit, I have been thinking about getting a new car. Our old one is starting to have too many issues. What do you think?"

Ajit: "I agree, Ratna. It is time for an upgrade. Let us look at our savings and see what we can afford."

Ratna: "I was thinking of setting a budget of $20,000. We can also consider financing options if needed."

Ajit: "That sounds reasonable. Let us research different models and see which ones fit our budget. We should also check for any ongoing deals or discounts."

Ratna: "Great idea! We can visit a few dealerships this weekend and test drive some cars. I am excited to find the perfect one. I work for the bank and can manage a loan due to my long service with them."

Reflection: Ratna and Ajit's conversation highlights their collaborative approach to making a major purchase, ensuring they stay within their budget while considering all options.

Example 3: Addressing Financial Concerns

Scenario: Bertie and Alina are discussing their financial concerns.

Alina: "Bertie, I have been feeling a bit stressed about our finances lately. Can we talk about it?"

Bertie: "Of course, Alina, what's been on your mind?"

Alina: "I am worried about our credit card debt. It has been growing, and I'm not sure how we'll pay it off."

Bertie: "I understand your concern. Let us create a plan to tackle the debt. We can start by cutting down on non-essential expenses and putting that money towards our credit card payments."

Alina: "That sounds like a good plan. We can also investigate balance transfer options to reduce the interest rate."

Bertie: "Absolutely. We will get through this together. Let us set up a meeting with a financial advisor to get some professional advice."

Reflection: Bertie and Alina's conversation demonstrates their willingness to address financial concerns openly and work together to find solutions.

Example 4: Setting Financial Goals

Reuben and Neha are setting their financial goals for the year.

Reuben: "Neha, I think it's time we set some financial goals for this year. What do you think?"

Neha "I agree, Reuben Let's start by listing our short-term and long-term goals."

Reuben: "For short-term goals, I'd like to save for a vacation and pay off our student loans."

Neha: "Those are great goals. For long-term, we should focus on building our emergency fund and saving for a down payment on a house."

Reuben: "Perfect. Let us create a timeline for each goal and track our progress regularly."

Neha: "I love it! We can also reward ourselves when we achieve each milestone. It will keep us motivated."

Reflection: Reuben and Neha's conversation shows their proactive approach to setting and achieving financial goals, ensuring they stay on track and celebrate their successes.

Relevant Proverbs and Quotes

- "A penny saved is a penny earned." – Benjamin Franklin

- "The art is not in making money, but in keeping it." – Proverb

- "Financial peace isn't the acquisition of stuff. It is learning to live on less than you make so you can give money back and have money to invest. You can't win until you do this." – Dave Ram

Activities and Reflections

- Activity: Create a monthly budget together and review it at the end of each month.

- Reflection: Discuss how budgeting has impacted your financial situation and relationship. What adjustments can you make for the next month?

- Open communication: have honest discussion about your financial situation, desire to work or not and transparency on all financial matters.

- Set Boundaries: Establish clear boundaries regarding financial behaviours, such as not lending money for gambling or setting limits on spending.

- Seek Help: If gambling addiction or excessive debt is already an issue, seek professional help before settling down into a marriage. Financial counselling and therapy can provide the necessary support to manage these problems effectively.

Activity: Financial Planning for Your Wedding

Step 1: **Reflective Journaling**

1. **Set the Scene**: Find a quiet and comfortable space where you can reflect without distractions. Have a journal or a piece of paper and a pen ready.

2. **Prompt Questions:** Write down and answer the following questions in your journal:

   o What is my current financial situation, including income, savings, debts, and expenses?

   o What are my short-term and long-term financial goals?

   o What is our spending and saving habits?

   o What is my credit score, and what does my credit report look like?

   o How do I feel about cultural traditions like dowry? Do I see them as meaningful practice or a burden?

Step 2: Partner Discussion

1. **Share Your Reflections**: Take turns sharing your reflections with your partner. Listen actively and empathetically to each other's financial situations and goals.

2. **Ask Open-Ended Questions**: Encourage deeper conversation by asking open-ended questions such as:

- o What are your financial goals for the next five years?
- o How do you feel about our current financial situation?
- o What are your thoughts on budgeting for our wedding?
- o How can we support each other in achieving our financial goals?
- o How do you feel about cultural traditions like dowry? How should we approach them?

3. **Create a Wedding Budget**: Work together to create a detailed budget for your wedding. Discuss how you will save money for the wedding and manage expenses.

Conclusion

Having conversations about your financial status and how you will finance your wedding is a vital step in building a strong and committed relationship. These discussions can help you understand each other's financial situations, align your goals, and create a shared vision for your future together. Embrace this journey with openness and honesty, and let these conversations deepen your connection and mutual understanding.

References:

Pew Research Centre. (2022). Most in the U.S. say young adults today face more challenges than their parents' generation in some key areas. Retrieved from Pew Research Centre

Maritz, C. (2023). Teenagers, love, challenges, and problems. Retrieved from Christel Maritz Psychologist

In many Middle Eastern cultures, dowry is considered a legal right for women and is mandatory at Islamic weddings (Pew Research Centre, 2022).

The dowry system in India, despite being outlawed, continues to influence wedding practices and can include substantial contributions such as cash, gold, and household items (Maritz, 2023).

Gaspard, T. (n.d.). Talking About Finances: A Touchy Topic Made Easier for Couples. Retrieved from Gottman Institute.

Alberhasky, M. (2023). How to Discuss Money in a Romantic Relationship. Retrieved from Psychology Today.

American Psychological Association. (2015). Happy couples: How to avoid money arguments. Retrieved from APA.

Chapter 5

Welcoming New Bonds: Introducing Your Partner to Family

In this chapter, we delve into the delicate and significant process of introducing your partner to your family, particularly your in-laws. We explore the dynamics of merging two families, understanding the expectations and traditions that come with it, and the importance of creating a harmonious environment for these new relationships to flourish.

"Remember, your parents only know what you share with them. If you turn to them every time, you are angry, frustrated, or facing marital issues, they hear those moments. But they do not hear about the times you make up and find happiness again."

"In every marriage, six souls intertwine,
Two become one, their histories align.
We choose to mesh or let pasts collide,
In love's embrace, or in shadows we hide."

Introduction

The topic of in-laws often comes with a lot of hype and negative press. However, it is important to note that when 50 percent of marriages or relationships break up, it is rarely due to the involvement of in-laws. While it may not always be possible to get along with every member of your partner's family, having a great relationship with your in-laws can be one of the greatest blessings to your marriage. Positive in-law relationships are achievable and beneficial overall. Introducing your partner to your family, especially your in-laws, is a significant step in your relationship. This process can be both exciting and challenging, as it involves merging divergent backgrounds, traditions, and expectations. Here is how you can navigate this journey together:

Navigating Family Introductions: Building Bridges for a Harmonious Future

Introducing your partner to your family is a significant step that requires careful preparation and thoughtful communication. Imagine Elvis and Colette, who are about to embark on this journey. They understand the importance of setting the right expectations and making everyone feel comfortable and respected.

Preparation and Communication

Before the big introduction, Elvis and Colette sit down to share vital details about each other with their families. Colette tells her parents about Elvis' background, his interests, and what she loves about him. Ben does the same with his family. This preparation helps set the right expectations and ensures that everyone is on the same page. Clear communication is key to making everyone feel at ease.

First Impressions

Making a positive first impression is crucial. On the day of the introduction, Elvis and Colette approach the meeting with grace and respect. Elvis brings a small gift for Colette's parents as a gesture of goodwill, and Sarah makes sure to show genuine interest in Ben's family, asking questions and being polite. These simple gestures go a long way in building a solid foundation for their relationship with each other's families.

Building Bridges

Fostering mutual understanding and respect between Colette, Elvis, and their families is essential. During their visit, they emphasize the importance of empathy and open-mindedness. Colette encourages her parents to share stories about their family traditions, and Ben does the same with his family. This exchange of stories and traditions creates a sense of connection and appreciation, helping both families feel more comfortable and connected.

Managing Conflicts

Conflicts or misunderstandings may arise, and that is okay. When a small disagreement occurs about a cultural tradition, **Colette and Elvis** address it constructively. They listen to each other's perspectives and find common ground. "It's about building a harmonious relationship, not winning an argument," Colette reminds everyone. This approach helps diffuse tension and foster a spirit of cooperation.

Creating New Traditions

Blending family traditions can be a beautiful experience. **Elvis and Colette** decide to create new traditions that honour both their backgrounds. They plan to host a combined family dinner every holiday season, where they incorporate dishes and customs from both families. This strengthens their bond and creates lasting memories.

Respect Across Generations

Understanding that perspectives on family unity and independence can vary, **Elvis and Colette** respect each other's family values while navigating their own path. They recognize that some may prioritize immediate family well-being over traditional expectations, much like Prince Harry did. However, they strive to maintain family bonds while respecting these choices, understanding the importance of seeing the bigger picture.

Traditional vs. Modern Family Dynamics

When traditional family values meet modern lifestyles, challenges can arise. **Elvis and Colette**, these differences by fostering respect and understanding between generations. They engage in open dialogue and compromise to bridge any gaps, ensuring that both traditional and modern values are honoured.

Inter-Racial and Cultural Harmony

Ali and Yen's relationship is inter-racial and intercultural, bringing unique challenges. They overcome potential disharmony by fostering a respectful and inclusive family environment. They celebrate cultural diversity and find common ground, strengthening their family bonds and creating a rich, blended family culture.

Respect

You might be thinking, "But wait, you don't understand. They have treated me badly in the past, or they don't like me." Unfortunately, that happens. But let us consider relationships. You love your spouse, don't you? They must have qualities that drew you to them. How did they become the person they are? Their parents played a significant role in shaping them. They loved their child and taught them how to be a good person, instilling the qualities you love. Someone who did that for the person I love deserves my respect at the very least and my love at the most. Because I love my spouse and want to show that to them, I am willing to recognize how important their parents are to them and to act kindly towards them.

The Challenge

If you do not have a good relationship with your in-laws right now, I challenge you to change your habits towards them. Be thoughtful and kind. Treat them as you would like others to treat your parents. Remember, they raised the most important person in the world to you. They must be good people!

The In-Laws

If you have in-laws who do not respect your marriage, I am not asking you to expose yourself or your relationship to criticism or abuse. However, if you take the first steps in ending the bickering, you might find people who are open to having a relationship with you. As a parent with two married children, my biggest concern in their marriages is that their spouses treat my kids well. If my kids are happy in their marriage, then I am happy to open my heart and our family to their spouse.

By following these guidelines, Ali and Yen navigate the complexities of introducing each other to their families. They foster strong and positive relationships that contribute to a supportive and loving family environment. Remember, the goal is to build bridges, not walls, and to create a harmonious blend of traditions and values. By the end of their journey, they have a comprehensive understanding of how to foster strong and positive relationships, ensuring a supportive and loving family environment.

Activity: Reflect and Act

1. **Reflection:** Take a moment to reflect on the qualities you love in your spouse. Write down how their parents might have contributed to these qualities.

2. **Action:** Plan a small act of kindness for your in-laws. It could be a thoughtful message, a small gift, or offering help with something they need.

"Respect is one of the greatest expressions of love." — Miguel Angel Ruiz

Conversations with Self Expectations and Boundaries

Before introducing your partner to your in-laws, it is essential to have a conversation with yourself about your expectations and boundaries. Reflect on the following questions:

- What are your expectations for this meeting?

- What boundaries do you need to set to ensure a respectful and comfortable interaction?

- How do you envision the relationship between your partner and your in-laws?

Challenges Couples Face When Introducing Their Partner to In-Laws

Introducing your partner to your in-laws can be a nerve-wracking experience. Here are some familiar challenges couples face:

1. **Cultural Differences:** Navigating diverse cultural backgrounds and traditions.

2. **Expectations:** Managing the expectations of both your partner and your in-laws.

3. **First Impressions:** Ensuring a positive first impression while being authentic.

4. **Communication Styles:** Bridging different communication styles and preference.

Activity: Role-Playing the Introduction

1. **Set the Scene:** Imagine the setting where the introduction will take place. It could be a family dinner, a casual get-together, or a formal event.

2. **Assign Roles:** One person plays the role of the in-laws, and the other plays the role of the partner.

3. **Practice Scenarios:** Go through different scenarios, such as:

   o Introducing your partner to your parents.

   o Answering frequent questions about your relationship.

   o Overseeing potential conflicts or misunderstandings.

4. **Switch Roles:** After practicing, switch roles to gain different perspectives.

Conversation 1: Meeting the In-Laws for the First Time

Dinky: "I'm nervous about meeting your parents this weekend. What if they do not like me?"

Joel: "I understand how you feel. I was nervous when I met your parents too. Just be yourself. They'll love you because I love you."

Dinky: "What are they like? Any tips on what I should or should not do?"

Joel: "My parents are very acceptable and amicable. Just be respectful and show interest in getting to know them. Maybe ask about their hobbies or how they met. They love sharing stories."

Dinky: "Okay, I can do that. Thanks for the advice. I just want to make a good impression."

Joel: "You will. And remember, I am here with you all the way. We'll get through this together."

Conversation 2: Dealing with Past Conflicts

Bobby: "I know your mom and I haven't always seen eye-to-eye, but I want to improve our relationship. Any suggestions?"

Mishael: "I appreciate that, Bobby. Maybe start by finding common ground. She loves gardening, and I know you've been interested in starting a garden."

Bobby: "That's a good idea. I could ask her for some tips. I just want her to see that I care about you and our family."

Mishael: "She'll appreciate the effort. And remember, it takes time. Just keep being kind and patient."

Bobby: "Thanks, Mishael. I will try it. I really want us all to get along."

Conversation 3: Setting Boundaries

Clarence: "Your parents have been dropping by unannounced a lot lately. It's starting to feel a bit overwhelming."

Merl: "I didn't realize it was bothering you so much. Let's talk to them together and set some boundaries."

Clarence: "I think that would help. We can suggest they call before coming over?"

Merl: "Absolutely. We can explain that we need some notice to prepare and that it's not about them, but about us needing our space."

Clarence: "I hope they understand. I just want to make sure we have our own time too."

Merl: "They will. They love us and want us to be happy. We'll handle this together."

Conversation 4: Appreciating In-Laws

Skye: "Your dad was so helpful with fixing the sink today. I really appreciate his help."

Valdon: "He loves being useful. It makes him happy to help us out."

Skye: "I should bake him some cookies as a thank you. Do you think he would like that?"

Valdon: "He'd love that. It's a great way to show your appreciation."

Skye: "I want him to know that I value his support. It means a lot to me."

Valdon: "He'll be touched. It's little gestures like this that strengthen our family bonds."

These conversations illustrate the importance of communication, respect, and effort in building and maintaining positive in-law relationships. For couples living on their own, these dialogues can be quite useful. However, in traditional and joint family situations, conversations might look different. If serious problems arise, counselling and family mediation can be beneficial. It's crucial for each party to take responsibility where change is necessary and accept each other's differences.

Conversation 1: Traditional Chinese Family

Li Wei: "Mei, I know living with my parents can be challenging at times, but it's important to me. They've always been there for us."

Mei: "I understand, Li Wei. I respect your parents and appreciate everything they do for us. But sometimes, I feel like we don't have enough privacy."

Li Wei: "I get that. Maybe we can set some boundaries to ensure we have our own space while still being respectful to them."

Mei: "That sounds like a good idea. How about we have a weekly family dinner where we all spend time together but also make sure we have our own time in the evenings?"

Li Wei: "I think that's a great compromise. I will talk to my parents about it. They'll understand if we explain it's for the benefit of our relationship."

Mei: "Thank you, Li Wei. I want us to have a harmonious home where everyone feels respected and valued."

Conversation 2: Traditional Indian Family

Harwant: "Sapna, I know my parents can be a bit overbearing sometimes, but they mean well. They just want to be involved in our lives."

Sapna: "I know, Harwant. I respect them a lot, but it can be overwhelming when they make decisions without consulting us."

Harwant: "I agree. We can have a family meeting and discuss how we can all work together better. We can explain that while we value their input, we also need to make some decisions on our own."

Sapna: "That's a good idea. We can suggest having regular family discussions where everyone can share their thoughts, and we can make decisions together."

Harwant: "Yes, and we can also set some boundaries about our personal space and time. It's important for us to have our own moments too."

Sapna: "Absolutely. I think if we communicate openly and respectfully, we can find a balance that works for everyone."

Harwant: "I'll talk to my parents. I'm sure they'll understand if we explain it's for the good of our relationship and the family."

These conversations highlight the importance of open communication, setting boundaries, and finding compromises in joint family situations. They can help couples navigate the complexities of living with extended family while maintaining their own relationship dynamics.

References

☐ Anderson, D. A., & Sabatelli, R. M. (2010). *Family communication: Theory, research, and practice* (4th ed.). McGraw-Hill.

☐ Doherty, W. J. (2005). *The family relationship inventory: A measure of family-of-origin experiences. Journal of Family Therapy, 27*(3), 253-271. https://doi.org/10.1111/j.1467-6427.2005.00292.x

☐ Knudson, M. M., & Segrin, C. (2014). *Family communication patterns and relational satisfaction: The mediating role of family cohesion and adaptability. Journal of Family Communication, 14*(1), 1-15. https://doi.org/10.1080/15267431.2013.856491

☐ Markman, H. J., & Stanley, S. M. (2006). *Families and family therapy: An introduction.* Sage Publications.

☐ Whitchurch, E. G., & Constantine, L. L. (2009). *Integrating family therapy and multiculturalism: A contextual approach. Journal of Marital and Family Therapy, 35*(1), 3-16. https://doi.org/10.1111/j.1752-0606.2008.00099.x

Module 2
The Honeymoon Phase and Beyond: Challenges in Early Marriage

Chapter 1

Harmony at home: As tasks to strengths, we divide!

This chapter delves into the art of creating a harmonious home by dividing tasks according to each partner's strengths. It emphasizes the importance of recognizing and valuing each other's abilities, fostering a sense of teamwork and mutual respect. By aligning tasks with individual strengths, couples can enhance efficiency, reduce stress, and build a supportive and balanced household. This chapter offers practical advice on how to have these conversations and implement effective strategies for task division.

"The greatest marriages are built on teamwork. A mutual respect, a healthy dose of admiration, and a never-ending portion of love and grace. — **Fawn Weaver**

Harmony at home, as tasks to strengths we divide,

In unity and balance, our love and lives abide.

With every chore and duty, we find our rhythm true,

Together, we make this better in all we say and do.

Introduction

Managing household tasks is a fundamental aspect of living together, whether as a couple, family, or roommates. The division of these tasks can often be a source of tension, but it also presents an opportunity to build teamwork and strengthen relationships. By approaching household chores with a spirit of cooperation and mutual respect, couples can create a harmonious living environment. Gender roles are no longer the norm in these current times when both partners are working full time, have jobs, and have gardens, lawns, and huge houses to tend to. It is imperative to have all tasks divided by likes, dislikes, strengths, and ones that bring about a give-and-take balance. Enjoy the art of giving! Marriages thrive on this aspect when we apply it to all aspects. It is not all about being loved; it's wanting to give, which strikes gold. Before we begin the journey, let us understand what happens when couples first start living together.

The Honeymoon Phase and Beyond: Navigating Early Marriage Challenges

When Veneta and Dexter exchanged their vows, they could not wait to embark on their life together. The honeymoon phase was magical, filled with excitement, romance, and the joy of being newlyweds. However, as the initial euphoria began to settle, they soon realized that the journey of marriage comes with its own set of challenges.

The First Steps: Building Strong Foundations

In the first few months, Veneta and Dexter were learning to merge their individual lives into one. They discovered that building a solid foundation required effort and patience. "We need to establish our routines and find a balance between our personal and shared time," Veneta suggested. They decided to dedicate their weekends to exploring new activities together while maintaining their personal hobbies during the weekdays.

Financial Adjustments

One of the first hurdles they faced was managing finances. Veneta and Dexter had different spending habits. Dexter was a saver, while Veneta enjoyed occasional splurges. They decided to create a budget together. "Let's set aside an amount for savings and some for fun activities," Dexter proposed. This compromise helped them manage their finances without sacrificing their individual preferences.

Communication is Key

Open and honest communication was another crucial aspect of navigating early marriage. Misunderstandings were inevitable, but how they managed them made all the difference. After a minor disagreement about household chores, Sam expressed, "I feel overwhelmed when I have to do all the cleaning." Veneta replied, "I didn't realize it was too much for you. Let's divide the chores and create a schedule." This approach fostered understanding and cooperation.

Balancing Family and Personal Time

Balancing time between family visits and personal moments was another challenge. Both sets of parents were eager to spend time with the newlyweds.

"We need to find a way to balance time with our families and our alone time," Veneta suggested. They decided to designate certain weekends for family visits and others for just the two of them, ensuring a healthy balance.

Handling Conflicts

Conflicts are a natural part of any relationship. Veneta and Dexter learned to address disagreements constructively by listening to each other's perspectives and finding common ground. "It's not about who wins the argument but about finding a solution that works for both of us," Dexter reminded Veneta during a heated discussion. This mindset helped them navigate conflicts with empathy and mutual respect.

Creating Shared Traditions

Creating shared traditions became a beautiful experience for Sam and Lily. They decided to blend their family traditions and create new ones unique to their relationship. "How about we host a combined family dinner every holiday season?" Veneta suggested. This idea allowed them to honour both backgrounds while building lasting memories.

Respecting Individual Growth

Understanding that each partner continues to grow individually is vital. Veneta and Dexter supported each other's personal goals and aspirations. "I want to pursue a course in graphic design," Veneta shared. Dexter encouraged her, "Go for it! I'll support you every step of the way." This mutual respect for each other's growth strengthened their bond.

Overcoming Challenges Together

The first year of marriage was filled with learning and adjustments, but Sam and Lily faced each challenge hand in hand. They recognized that the key to a successful marriage was not avoiding problems but navigating them together with love, patience, and understanding.

Moving Forward

As they moved beyond the honeymoon phase, Veneta and Dexter realized that marriage is a journey of continuous growth and discovery. They were committed to building a strong, supportive, and loving relationship, ready to face any challenge that came their way.

By understanding and addressing these early marriage challenges, couples like Veneta and Dexter can strengthen their relationship, ensuring a solid foundation for a lifetime of love and partnership.

The Importance of Teamwork in Household Management: Sharing household responsibilities is more than just dividing chores; it's about fostering a sense of partnership and mutual respect. When both partners contribute to maintaining the home, it demonstrates a commitment to equality and fairness. This shared responsibility can enhance communication, reduce stress, and create a more balanced and satisfying relationship.

Communication and Planning: Effective communication is key to managing household tasks. Couples should discuss their preferences, strengths, and schedules to create a fair division of labour. Regular check-ins and planning sessions can help ensure that tasks are distributed equitably and that both partners feel valued and supported.

Creating a Chore Schedule: A chore schedule can be a practical tool for managing household tasks by clearly outlining who is responsible for what and when couples can avoid misunderstandings and ensure that all necessary tasks are completed. Flexibility is important, as schedules may need to be adjusted based on changing circumstances.

Recognizing and Appreciating Contributions: Acknowledging each other's efforts is crucial. Simple gestures of appreciation can go a long way in maintaining a positive atmosphere whether it's a thank you note or a verbal acknowledgment, showing gratitude for each other's contributions reinforces a sense of teamwork and mutual respect.

Addressing Imbalances: If one partner feels overwhelmed or that the division of labour is unfair, it is important to address these concerns openly and constructively. Discussing and adjusting the distribution of tasks can help prevent resentment and ensure that both partners feel supported.

Conversation 1: Establishing a Chore Schedule

Roy: "Hey, Cris, we need to talk about our household chores. I feel like things have been a bit chaotic lately."

Cris: "I agree, Roy, things are just getting shelved. However, with my new managerial post, I am working later hours. What do you suggest?"

Roy: "How about we create a tasks schedule? We can list all the tasks and divide them based on our preferences and availability, and on the days you work late, I will manage the cooking. However, you can complete the other household tasks on the weekends. Does that sound fair?"

Cris: "That sounds like a good idea. Let's sit down this weekend and work on it together." "And maybe the tasks that are not getting done, we can afford some hired help."

Roy: "Great! This way, we can make sure everything gets done without one of us feeling overwhelmed."

Roy and Cris both work full-time jobs and often find it challenging to keep up with household chores. They decided to sit down and discuss how they could divide the tasks more evenly. By creating a chore/task chart and setting aside specific times for cleaning, they were able to manage their responsibilities better and reduce stress. Due to their high-pressure managerial positions, they decided to have a cleaner and gardener twice a month.

Conversation 2: Addressing Imbalances

Gwen: "Darrell, I have been feeling really stressed about all the housework lately. I think we need to re-evaluate our chore distribution."

Darrell: "I am sorry to hear that, Gwen. I did not realize you were feeling this way. Let us talk about it. We spoke for a while about getting laundry services and home-delivered meals during the mid-week period, as with kids and their schooling, it does get difficult having our full-time work careers and then helping the kids with their schoolwork, dropping and picking up. It might be best to give ourselves a reprieve for just 3 days of the week. That way, we would not be so burdened and could relax for a few hours on the weekend.

Gwen: "that is a great idea, and yes, much that I enjoy cooking; getting home-cooked and home-delivered meals mid-week sounds very much like a treat and giving the uniforms and work clothes for ironing takes so off some drudgery from the routine. I understand this will be only until something for us eases."

Darrell "Absolutely. Let us make a list of all the balance chores and see how we can divide them more fairly."

Gwen enjoys cooking, while Darrell enjoys cleaning the house. They agreed to take on these tasks based on their preferences, which made the chores feel less burdensome. By playing to their strengths, they found a way to make household tasks more enjoyable. However, with growing family needs, they have also treated themselves to having chores outsourced. This helps them not to have to cook 5 days a week and save on restaurant bills, but also know this would help them find some time for a balance and enjoy themselves.

Conversation 3: Recognizing Contributions

Clint: "Charls, I just wanted to say thank you for taking care of the laundry this week. I really appreciate it."

Charls: "Thanks, Clint. I noticed you've been managing the cooking, and it's been a huge help."

Clint: "I am glad we can support each other. It makes managing everything so much easier."

Charls: "Definitely. Let us keep communicating and appreciating each other's efforts."

Charls and Clint have deep respect and gratitude for one another and make it a point to give daily affirmations to one another in their conversations.

Activity: Reflect and Act

Reflection: Take some time to reflect on your current division of household tasks. Are there any areas where you feel overwhelmed or unsupported? Write down your thoughts and discuss them with your partner.

Action: Create a chore schedule together. List all the household tasks and divide them based on your preferences and availability. Make sure to include regular check-ins to adjust the schedule as needed.

Self-Reflections

Personal Contributions: Reflect on the tasks you currently manage and how they contribute to the household. Are there any tasks you enjoy or excel at?

Support Systems: Identify ways you and your partner can support each other in managing household tasks. This might include sharing responsibilities or offering help when one of you is overwhelmed.

Future Planning: Think about how you can maintain a fair and balanced division of labour as your circumstances change. Discuss these plans with your partner to ensure you are both aligned.

Conclusion

Managing household tasks effectively requires teamwork, communication, and mutual respect. By approaching these responsibilities with a spirit of cooperation, couples can create a harmonious and supportive living environment. Regularly discussing and adjusting the division of labour ensures that both partners feel valued and supported, leading to a stronger and more satisfying relationship.

References

Psychology Today discusses the importance of sharing home and life responsibilities with your partner1.

Marriage.com highlights the benefits of sharing household duties for a happier marriage2.

Amenify explores the advantages of sharing house chores and how it fosters better relationships3.

Veronica Hanson provides strategies for managing household responsibilities fairly and effectively4.

Driskell, J. E., Salas, E., & Driskell, T. (2018). Foundations of teamwork and collaboration. American Psychologist, 73(4), 334–348. https://doi.org/10.1037/amp0000241

Weir, K. (2018, September 1). What makes teams work? Monitor on Psychology, 49(8). Retrieved from https://www.apa.org/monitor/2018/09/cover-teams

Chapter 2

Unveiling Intimacy with Sensitivity: Expectations, Needs, and Inhibitions

This chapter explores the multifaceted nature of intimacy within relationships, delving into the expectations, needs, and inhibitions that partners may experience. It emphasizes the importance of open and honest communication to navigate these sensitive topics. By understanding and addressing each other's desires and boundaries, couples can foster a deeper connection and a more fulfilling intimate life. The chapter provides practical advice on how to discuss intimate expectations, recognize and respect each other's needs, and overcome inhibitions together. Through empathy and mutual support, partners can create a safe and loving space for intimacy to thrive.

"Intimacy is not purely physical. It is the act of connecting with someone so deeply, you feel like you can see into their soul."

*Sex can be renounced, but sexuality remains
A vital part of who we are, in joys and pains.
We cannot avoid these issues by turning
away or dismissing their importance, come
what may.*

*Respect your feelings and those of others,
too, for in understanding and empathy, love
will renew. In the dance of intimacy, let
honesty be your guide, Together, face the
truths that within you reside.*

Introduction:

Sexuality is a fundamental aspect of intimate relationships, yet it can often be a source of confusion, frustration, and conflict. Open and honest conversations about sexual issues, expectations, incompetency, needs, and inhibitions are crucial for maintaining a healthy and fulfilling relationship. By addressing these topics, couples can enhance their intimacy, build trust, and ensure that both partners' needs are met. Many relationships can stop being unfulfilling and resorting to means that could be detrimental to the marriage or the relationship.

The Importance of Discussing Sexual Issues

Understanding the Importance of Discussing Sexual Issues

Meet Laura and Mike, a couple who have been together for five years. They love each other deeply but recently noticed a growing distance in their relationship. One evening, over a cozy dinner at home, Laura mentions a topic that has been on her mind.

"Mike, I have been feeling like our intimacy isn't what it used to be. Can we talk about it?"

Mike, slightly surprised but willing, nods. "Sure, Laura. I have been feeling it too. Let's figure this out together."

Enhanced Intimacy

Laura and Mike's openness leads them to discuss their needs and desires candidly. Laura shares her need for more emotional connection, while Mike expresses his interest in trying new things in their intimate life. This conversation not only helps them understand each other better but also brings them closer, both emotionally and physically.

Improved Communication

As they talk, Laura and Mike realize that discussing sexual issues fosters better communication overall. They begin to feel more comfortable expressing their thoughts and concerns, which helps in resolving other conflicts and misunderstandings that arise in their relationship.

Increased Satisfaction

Addressing their sexual expectations and needs leads to greater satisfaction for both. Laura feels more cherished and emotionally fulfilled, while Mike feels more connected and valued. Their overall relationship happiness increases as a result.

Reduced Anxiety

Mike admits to Laura that he sometimes feels insecure about his performance. Laura, with empathy in her eyes, reassures him. "I love you for who you are, Mike. We're in this together." This honest exchange reduces Mike's anxiety and builds his confidence, strengthening their bond.

Barriers to Communication

Despite their progress, Laura, and Mike face barriers in their communication journey. Laura sometimes fears rejection, and Mike struggles with stress from work. Cultural norms have also played a role in their hesitancy to discuss these topics openly.

Emotional Barriers

Laura's fear of rejection sometimes makes her hold back her true feelings. One evening, Mike notices she is quieter than usual and gently asks, "Laura, what's on your mind?"

Laura sighs, "I am afraid that if I share my needs, you might think less of me."

Mike takes her hand, "Never. Your feelings matter to me. Please share what's on your mind."

Cultural and Societal Norms

Both Laura and Mike grew up in environments, where talking about sex was taboo. This societal stigma had seeped into their relationship, making open discussions challenging.

Gender Roles

Mike sometimes feels pressured to conform to traditional gender roles, believing he must always be the strong, silent type. Laura helps him break free from this by encouraging vulnerability.

Personal Inhibitions

Laura's past experiences and low self-esteem sometimes hinder her from expressing her needs. Mike reassures her, "Laura, your feelings are important. You deserve to have your needs met."

Lack of Communication Skills

Sometimes, they struggle to articulate their feelings or misinterpret each other's words. They decide to improve their communication skills together.

Overcoming Barriers

Laura and Mike embark on a journey to overcome these barriers. They create a safe, non-judgmental space for dialogue, where they practice active listening. Building trust and empathy becomes their focus, with each showing consistent support.

Creating a Safe Space

One weekend, they set aside time for an uninterrupted heart-to-heart. "Let's make this our safe space, where we can share anything without fear," Laura suggests.

Building Trust and Empathy

They show empathy by acknowledging and validating each other's feelings. When Mike shares his insecurities, Laura responds with warmth and understanding, building trust between them.

Improving Communication Skills

Laura and Mike practice using "I" statements to express their feelings without blaming each other. "I feel neglected when we don't spend quality time together," Laura says softly.

Mike nods, "I understand. Let's make more time for us."

Seeking Professional Help

They realize that they might need external guidance and decide to see a therapist. The therapist helps them improve their communication and address underlying issues.

Education and Awareness

Laura and Mike educate themselves about each other's needs and preferences through books and workshops. They also respect cultural differences and work towards a more understanding relationship.

By addressing these barriers and implementing these strategies, Laura and Mike enhance their communication, deepen their connection, and navigate sensitive topics with greater ease and understanding.

Dialogues

1. **Anjali and Ronnie**: Anjali felt uncomfortable discussing her sexual needs with Ronnie, even after they were married. She often struggled with her constrictive upbringing and could not express herself. However, Ronnie persevered and, with deep sensitivity and understanding, helped her unpack her feelings a little at a time.

Ronnie: "Anjali, I understand that your parents and upbringing did not allow you to talk about sex and the matters relating. However, it is important I know how you feel".

Anjali: "Yes, Ronnie, it is indeed difficult for me, and I do feel very restrained, but I will try to do my best.

Ronnie: "Take your time and let me know how I can help. All I want is for us both to have a fulfilling life."

Anjali: "It's so comforting to hear you speak in this way, and I will surely start one day at a time. In the meantime, I am also getting help from a counsellor. She helps me with assertive and expressive communication and working with my family of origin issues.

Bruce and Viola: Bruce struggled with sexual performance anxiety, which affected their intimacy. Viola suggested they see a therapist together to address the issue. Through counselling, they learned techniques to manage anxiety and enhance their sexual connection.

Viola: "Dear Bruce, at your request, I have booked an appointment with a Sex therapist who has come through incredibly good references, and we have an appointment next week. How are you feeling about it?

Bruce: "Yes, I know I have been procrastinating about this issue, and I am glad you have taken the initiative; it is important I get help. It will help us both."

Viola: "That's really brave of you. Just know that according to our GP, this is common, and there are reliable results that can be expected.

Bruce: "Thank you, Viola. That is certainly reassuring and thank you for treating this so sensitively and without blame. I really appreciate your attitude and kindness; it is very encouraging."

Activity: Sexual Communication Exercise

Step 1: Set a Comfortable Environment

- Choose a private and comfortable setting where you can talk openly without interruptions.

Step 2: Use "I" Statements

- Express your feelings and needs using "I" statements to avoid sounding accusatory. For example, "I feel loved when we spend time being intimate."

Step 3: Listen Actively

- Listen to your partner without interrupting. Show empathy and understanding towards their feelings and concerns.

Step 4: Explore Together

- Discuss your sexual desires, fantasies, and any inhibitions. Be open to exploring innovative ideas and finding common ground.

Step 5: Seek Professional Help if Needed.

- If you encounter persistent issues, consider seeking the help of a sex therapist or counsellor.

Reflection

Reflect on the following questions:

- How did discussing sexual issues impact your relationship?

- What did you learn about your partner's needs and desires?

- How can you continue to maintain open communication about sexual matters?

Conclusion

Conversations about sexual issues, expectations, incompetence, needs, and inhibitions are essential for a healthy and fulfilling relationship. By addressing these topics openly and honestly, couples can enhance their intimacy, build trust, and ensure that both partners' needs are met. Remember, seeking professional help when needed can further support your journey towards a satisfying sexual relationship.

References

- Tolman, D. L., Diamond, L. M., Bauermeister, J. A., George, W. H., Pfaus, J. G., & Ward, L. M. (Eds.). (2014). APA handbook of sexuality and psychology, Vol. 2: Contextual approaches. American Psychological Association. https://doi.org/10.1037/14194-000

- Patterson, C. J., & D'Augelli, A. R. (Eds.). (2013). Handbook of psychology and sexual orientation. Oxford University Press.

- Veldhuis, C. B., Cascalheira, C. J., Delucio, K., Budge, S. L., Matsuno, E., Huynh, K., Puckett, J. A., Balsam, K. F., Velez, B. L., & Galupo, M. P. (2024). Sexual orientation and gender diversity research manuscript writing guide. Psychology of Sexual Orientation and Gender Diversity. Advance online publication. https://doi.org/10.1037/sgd0000722

- Meston, C. M., & Frohlich, P. F. (2000). The neurobiology of sexual function. Archives of General Psychiatry, 57, 1012-1030.

Chapter 3

Embracing In-Laws: Building Bridges, Not Barriers

This chapter focuses on the dynamics of integrating in-laws into a couple's life, transforming potential sources of tension into opportunities for connection and support. It explores the challenges and benefits of building positive relationships with in-laws, emphasizing the importance of empathy, communication, and mutual respect. The chapter provides practical advice on setting boundaries, managing expectations, and fostering a sense of inclusion. By embracing in-laws as part of the extended family, couples can create a more harmonious and supportive environment for everyone involved.

"In family life, love is the oil that eases friction, the cement that binds closer together, and the music that brings harmony." – Eva Burrows

When it comes to family, we have to strengthen old bonds to ensure the longevity of new ones. We have to believe in them with an open heart and mind. Our in-laws are allies, not outlaws out to get us. Work toward building bridges of love and drawing them near.

Through understanding and respect, bonds will grow, In the warmth of acceptance, relationships flow. Together we stand, as one

Introduction

Including in-laws in your life can enrich your relationship and create a stronger family bond. It requires effort, understanding, and open communication. By fostering positive relationships with your in-laws, you can build a supportive and loving extended family network.

The Usefulness and Benefits of Adding to Our Families

Integrating in-laws into your family can bring numerous benefits, enriching your lives in unexpected ways. Here are some key advantages:

1. **Expanded Support Network:**

   o Emotional Support: In-laws can provide additional emotional support during challenging times, offering different perspectives and advice.

   o Practical Help: They can assist with childcare, household tasks, and other responsibilities, easing the burden on the couple.

2. **Cultural and Generational Wisdom:**

   o Traditions and Values: In-laws can share valuable family traditions and cultural practices, enriching the family's heritage.

   o Life Experience: Their life experiences and wisdom can offer guidance and insights that benefit the younger generation.

3. **Strengthened Family Bonds:**

   o Unity and Cohesion: Embracing in-laws fosters a sense of unity and cohesion, creating a stronger, more resilient family unit.

   o Shared Celebrations: Including in-laws in family celebrations and milestones enhances the joy and significance of these events.

4. **Role Models for Children:**

   o Positive Relationships: Healthy relationships with in-laws can serve as positive role models for children, teaching them about respect, empathy, and cooperation.

   o Extended Family Love: Children benefit from the love and attention of a larger family network, contributing to their emotional well-being.

Examples

Example 1: Stacia and Selwyn

Stacia and Selwyn had been married for a few years when they realized that their relationship with Selwyn's parents was strained. Stacia felt uncomfortable around her in-laws, fearing judgment and criticism. Selwyn, recognizing the importance of family harmony, initiated a heartfelt conversation with Stacia about the benefits of building a better relationship with his parents.

Selwyn: "Stacia, I know my parents can be a bit overwhelming, but I believe we can find common ground. They have a lot of love to give, and I think we can benefit from their support."

Stacia: "I understand, Selwyn. I have been hesitant because I did not want to feel judged. But I see how important this is to you and our family."

Selwyn: Let us start by inviting them over for dinner more often. We can share our lives with them and show them how much we value their presence.

Over time, Selwyn's and Stacia's efforts paid off. They found that involving Selwyn's parents in their lives brought unexpected joy and support. Stacia felt more comfortable, and their children thrived with the additional love and attention they received from their grandparents.

Example 2: Linda and George

Linda and George faced challenges with Linda's mother, who often interfered in their decisions. This caused tension between Linda and George, as George felt his opinions were being overlooked. Understanding the need for balance, Linda decided to address the issue with her mother.

Linda: Mom, I love you and appreciate your advice, but George and I need to make our own decisions. We want you to be part of our lives, but I hope you understand that we need to set some boundaries.

Linda's Mother: I understand, Linda. I just want what is best for you both. I will try to step back and let you two lead and live your lives. After all, my advice is good-intentioned; however, each couple knows best what they need.

George: Thank you for understanding. We value your support and want you to be involved, but we also need space to grow as a couple.

By setting clear boundaries and communicating openly, Linda and George were able to improve their relationship with Linda's mother. She became a supportive presence rather than a source of conflict, and their family dynamic became more harmonious.

Ashley and Eva: Eva's parents lived far away, while Ashely's parents had passed away. They made conscious efforts to include friends and other distant relatives in their home so that their children did not miss extended family. They also made regular video calls to the close family members who lived abroad and always stayed connected. This helped maintain a close connection despite the distance.

Setting Boundaries with In-Laws

Meet Sarah and Jake, a couple navigating the complexities of setting boundaries with their in-laws. After a few challenging interactions, they realize the importance of establishing clear and respectful boundaries to maintain a healthy relationship.

One evening, Sarah turns to Jake, saying, "We need to talk about setting some boundaries with your parents. I think it's important for our relationship."

Jake nods, "I agree, Sarah. Let's make sure we're on the same page first, then we can communicate these boundaries clearly and respectfully to them."

Communicate Openly

Sarah and Jake sit down and discuss their boundaries, ensuring they understand each other's needs. They then plan a dinner with Jake's parents to share their thoughts. During the meal, Jake gently mentions the topic, "Mom, Dad, Sarah, and I have been discussing how we can all have more harmonious visits. We think it would help if we set some clear boundaries."

His parents, initially surprised, listen attentively. Sarah adds, "We value your visits, but we also need to ensure we have our own space."

Be Consistent

Over time, Sarah, and Jake stick to their boundaries, gently reminding Jake's parents when they overstep. This consistency helps enforce the limits they set, creating a more comfortable environment for everyone.

Respect Their Boundaries

Just as they set boundaries for themselves, Sarah and Jake make sure to respect Jake's parents' boundaries. They are mindful of their needs and preferences, which helps foster mutual respect and understanding.

Benefits of In-Laws as Babysitters

Sarah and Jake soon discover the benefits of having Jake's parents as babysitters. One evening, while preparing for a much-needed date night, Sarah expresses her appreciation, "It's so comforting to know our kids are in safe hands with your parents."

Jake smiles, "Yes, it's not only cost-effective but also strengthens the bond between our kids and their grandparents."

Their children, excited to spend time with their grandparents, look forward to these babysitting nights. Jake's parents enjoy the regular interaction, which helps reinforce family bonds.

Managing Troublesome In-Laws

However, not all in-law interactions are smooth. Sarah and Jake face various issues, but they tackle them with thoughtful strategies.

Overbearing In-Laws

Jake's mom often interferes in their personal decisions, offering unsolicited advice. One day, after another overwhelming conversation, Sarah suggests, "Maybe we should have a respectful conversation about needing our space."

Jake agrees, and during a calm moment, he says to his mom, "I feel overwhelmed when we receive a lot of advice. Can we try giving each other some more space?"

Distant In-Laws

Jake's dad, on the other hand, is emotionally distant. Sarah decides to bridge the gap by including him in family activities. "Let's invite your dad to our next family outing," she suggests.

Jake reaches out, and over time, his dad begins to open up, feeling more included and valued.

Judgmental In-Laws

Facing criticism about their lifestyle and career choices, Sarah and Jake decide to address it calmly. During a family gathering, Jake explains, "We appreciate your concern, but we've made these choices because they're what work best for us. We hope you can respect that."

Meddling In-Laws

When Jake's parents try to interfere in their financial decisions, Sarah and Jake present a united front. They politely but firmly decline unsolicited advice, explaining their need for autonomy.

Cultural or Generational Differences

Differences in cultural values lead to misunderstandings. Sarah and Jake take time to educate each other about their respective cultures, finding common ground and respecting each other's perspectives.

Activity: Planning Family Inclusion

Sarah and Jake want to ensure their in-laws feel included in their lives. They start by listing ways to include them, such as family dinners and holidays.

They create a schedule for regular activities involving their in-laws, like monthly dinners and weekend outings. Open communication plays a crucial role as they discuss their plans with Jake's parents, making sure they feel valued and included in the decision-making process.

Flexibility is key. They adjust their plans based on everyone's availability and preferences, maintaining positive relationships through mutual respect and understanding.

By setting boundaries, managing conflicts, and planning inclusive activities, Sarah and Jake foster a healthy, respectful, and harmonious relationship with their in-laws, benefiting their entire family.

Activity: Planning Family Inclusion

Step 1: Identify Opportunities for Inclusion

- List ways you can include your in-laws in your life, such as family dinners, holidays, and extraordinary events.

Step 2: Create a Schedule

- Plan regular activities or gatherings that involve your in-laws. This could be monthly dinners, weekend outings, or annual vacations.

Step 3: Communicate Openly

- Discuss your plans with your in-laws and get their input. Make sure they feel valued and included in the decision-making process.

Step 4: Be Flexible

- Be open to adjusting your plans based on everyone's availability and preferences. Flexibility is key to maintaining positive relationships.

Reflection

Reflect on the following questions:

- How did including your in-laws in your life impact your relationship with them?

- What challenges did you face, and how did you overcome them?

- How can you continue to foster positive relationships with your in-laws?

Conclusion

Including in-laws in your life can bring joy, support, and a sense of belonging. By making a conscious effort to involve them in your family activities, you can build stronger relationships and create a harmonious extended family. Remember, open communication and flexibility are essential in fostering these connections.

Quote for Inspiration:

"Family is not an important thing. It is everything." – Michael J. Fox

References

o Boss, P., & Greenberg, J. (1984). Women and their mothers-in-law: Triangles, ambiguity, and relationship quality. Social Work Research & Abstracts, 20(4), 259-270. https://doi.org/10.1093/swr/20.4.259

o Apostolou, M. (2021). In-law relationships in an evolutionary perspective: The good, the bad, and the ugly. Frontiers in Sociology, 6, 683501. https://doi.org/10.3389/fsoc.2021.683501

o Bryant, C. M., & Conger, R. D. (1999). The influence of in-laws on change in marital success. Journal of Marriage and Family, 61(2), 362-374. https://doi.org/10.2307/353756

o American Psychological Association. (2023). References. Retrieved from https://apastyle.apa.org/style-grammar-guidelines/references.

o Purdue Online Writing Lab. (n.d.). APA formatting and style guide (7th ed.). Retrieved from https://owl.purdue.edu/owl/research_and_citation/apa_style/apa_formatting _and_style_guide/index.html

Chapter 4

Strife to Strength: Healing and Growth Post-Conflict

Every relationship faces moments of conflict, where words wound and hearts ache. This book explores how couples can navigate these turbulent times and emerge even stronger. Through real-life stories and expert insights, you'll learn effective communication strategies, the art of apology, and ways to rebuild trust and intimacy. Transform conflict into a catalyst for deeper connection and understanding, proving that love's resilience can conquer even the toughest storms.

"The best way to mend a broken heart is time and mates." – Gwyneth Paltrow

In the eye of the storm, we may falter and fight, But from the ashes of conflict, love takes flight.
With words that heal and hearts laid bare, We grow through the struggle, a stronger pair.

Introduction

Conflicts are an inevitable part of any relationship. How couples manage these conflicts can significantly impact the strength and longevity of their relationship. By addressing issues constructively and working together to resolve them, couples can become stronger and more connected. This chapter explores strategies for maintaining a healthy coupleship after a conflict. Conflict is an inevitable element in intimate relationships, a crucible

63

through which the bonds of connection and intimacy are both assessed and strengthened. For couples

navigating these challenges, understanding the underlying psychological and emotional dynamics is crucial. This section delves into advanced theories and practical methodologies designed to facilitate resolution and foster resilience.

Psychological Underpinnings of Conflict

Conflict often stems from unmet needs and unresolved past experiences. Attachment theory posits that our early relationships with caregivers shape our expectations and behaviours in adult relationships. Anxious, avoidant, or secure attachment styles significantly influence how we perceive and respond to conflict. Couples can benefit from recognizing and discussing these patterns, allowing for more empathetic and constructive interactions.

Communication and Resolution Strategies

Effective Communication: At the heart of conflict resolution lies effective communication. Couples must strive for openness and honesty, employing "I" statements to express feelings without casting blame. For example, "I feel hurt when..." instead of "You always...".

Active Listening: Active listening involves fully focusing on, understanding, and responding to the partner's message. This includes validating their feelings, asking clarifying questions, and summarizing their points to ensure mutual understanding.

Repair Attempts: Repair attempts are crucial in de-escalating conflicts.

These can be verbal (apologies, affirmations) or non-verbal (hugging, smiling). Recognizing and accepting these gestures can significantly reduce tension and pave the way for resolution.

Exercises for Self-Reflection and Growth

Activity: The Emotional Bank Account: Visualize your relationship as an emotional bank account where positive interactions are deposits and negative interactions are withdrawals. Reflect on your recent exchanges and consider how you can make more deposits through kind acts, affirmations, and quality time.

Exercise: Attachment Styles Exploration: Reflect on your own attachment style and that of your partner. Discuss how this influences your interactions and develop strategies to support each other's needs more effectively.

Activity: Conflict Role-Play:

Engage in a role-play exercise where each partner takes turns voicing the other's perspective in a recent conflict. This can foster empathy and highlight underlying issues that might have been missed during the actual argument.

Self-Reflection Practices

Meet Nora and Russell, a couple dedicated to nurturing their relationship through self-reflection. They have discovered that certain practices, like journaling and mindfulness, can significantly enhance their connection and personal growth.

Journaling

Nora starts a new habit of journaling every night. She uses this time to process her emotions, document conflicts and their resolutions, and reflect on her personal growth. Russell joins her, and they sometimes share their entries. This practice helps them understand and articulate feelings that are difficult to express verbally. One evening, Nora writes about a recent argument and realizes how her own stress contributed to it. Sharing this with Russell brings them closer as they both reflect on their roles and how to avoid such conflicts in the future.

Mindfulness and Meditation

Russell introduces Nora to mindfulness and meditation. They incorporate these practices into their daily routine, cultivating a present-focused awareness that reduces reactivity and enhances emotional regulation. During a disagreement, Russell suggests, "Let's take a few minutes to meditate and calm down before we continue." This helps them approach conflicts with greater calmness and clarity.

By integrating journaling and mindfulness into their lives, Nora and Russell transform conflicts into opportunities for growth, deepening their connection and reinforcing their partnership's foundation.

Understanding and Addressing Common Conflict Sources

Nora and Russell learn about the common sources of conflict in relationships and how to address them.

Power Dynamics

They recognize that power imbalances can underlie many conflicts. To foster equality, they ensure both their voices are valued. They practice shared decision-making and rotate responsibilities to maintain balance. For instance, they take turns managing household chores and finances, ensuring that neither feels overwhelmed.

Emotional Intelligence

Both enhance their emotional intelligence by recognizing their own emotions and understanding each other's. They practice empathy, which helps bridge gaps in understanding and facilitate conflict resolution. During a tough conversation, Russell says, "I can see why you feel that way. Let's find a solution together."

Practical Conflict Resolution Techniques

Nora and Russell adopt practical techniques to resolve conflicts effectively.

Time-Outs

When arguments heat up, they implement structured time-outs. This involves pausing the discussion, calming down, and revisiting the issue with a clearer mind. One evening, during a heated debate, Nora suggests, "Let's take a break and cool off. We can talk about this again in an hour."

Check-Ins

They schedule regular emotional check-ins, maintaining awareness of each other's states and preventing conflicts from festering. These check-ins, whether weekly or daily, focus on sharing feelings and concerns. On Sunday nights, they discuss how they felt during the week and address any brewing issues.

Additional Activities and Exercises

Nora and Russell explore additional activities to strengthen their relationship.

Conflict Mapping

They visualize conflicts by mapping them out, identifying triggers, patterns, and underlying issues. This helps pinpoint recurring problems and devise targeted solutions. After a few sessions, they notice a pattern: most arguments happen when they are both tired. They decide to prioritize rest and adjust their schedules accordingly.

Strength-Based Exercises

They focus on each other's strengths rather than weaknesses. They write down what they appreciate about each other and share these lists, reinforcing positive aspects of their relationship amidst conflict. Nora writes, "Russell, I love how patient you are with the kids," while Russell notes, "Nora, your creativity always amazes me."

The Importance of Resolving Conflicts

Nora and Russell realize the crucial role of resolving conflicts in their relationship.

Emotional Healing

Resolving conflicts helps them in emotional healing, preventing resentment from building up. They make a habit of discussing and resolving issues promptly.

Strengthened Bond

Successfully navigating conflicts strengthens their bond, fostering trust and understanding. After each resolved conflict, they feel closer and more connected.

Improved Communication

Conflict resolution encourages open and honest communication, essential for a healthy relationship. They practice speaking openly about their feelings and listening to each other without judgment.

Personal Growth

Dealing with conflicts constructively promotes personal growth and self-awareness. Nora and Russell reflect on their behaviours, learning and growing from each experience.

How Conflicts Can Strengthen Relationships

Through their journey, Nora and Russell learn how conflicts can actually strengthen their relationship.

Deeper Understanding

Working through conflicts allows them to understand each other's perspectives and needs better, leading to a deeper connection.

Increased Resilience

Successfully resolving conflicts makes their relationship more resilient. They learn to navigate challenges together, strengthening their bond.

Enhanced Intimacy

Overcoming difficulties together enhances both emotional and physical intimacy. They feel more connected and supported.

Growth Opportunities

Conflicts provide opportunities for personal and relational growth. Emily and Jack develop better coping and communication skills, which benefit their relationship.

The Role of Counselling and Restorative Practices

When challenges feel insurmountable, Emily and Jack turn to counselling and restorative practices.

Couples Counselling

Counselling provides a safe space for them to explore their issues with the guidance of a trained professional. It helps them develop effective communication strategies, resolve conflicts, and rebuild trust.

Restorative Practices

These practices focus on repairing harm and restoring relationships through dialogue, empathy, and mutual understanding. They encourage Emily and Jack to address the root causes of conflicts and work collaboratively towards resolution.

By adopting these strategies and practices, Emily, and Jack transform conflicts into opportunities for growth, deepening their connection and reinforcing their partnership's foundation.

Examples of Conversations

1. **Eric and Tony:** After an intense argument about finances, Eric and Tony decided to take a break and cool down. Later, they sat down and discussed their concerns calmly, finding a compromise that worked for both. This approach helped them resolve the issue without lingering resentment.

2. **Maureen and Tim** had a disagreement about parenting styles. They agreed to seek the help of a family counsellor to mediate their discussions. This decision not only helped them resolve their conflict but also provided them with tools to overcome future disagreements more effectively.

Eric and Tony: Cooling Down and Compromising

Eric: "Tony, our argument earlier got really heated, and I need some time to cool down before we talk about finances again." Tony: "I understand. Let us take a break and revisit this later."

Later that day...

Eric: "Alright, I have had some time to think. I feel like we both have valid points, but we need a compromise that works for both of us." Tony: "I agree. Let us calmly discuss our concerns. My main issue is that we need to save more." Eric: "I see. For me, it is important to have some flexibility for occasional treats. How about we set a monthly budget that allows for both saving and some discretionary spending?" Tony: "That sounds fair. Let us try that for a few months and adjust if needed."

Maureen and Tim: Seeking Professional Help

Maureen: "Tim, we have been clashing over our parenting styles. We need help to find common ground."

Tim: "I have been thinking the same. Let us find a family counsellor to help us mediate this."

During the counselling session...

Counsellor: "Maureen, can you each share your perspectives on parenting?"

Maureen: "I believe in setting firm boundaries, but I worry Tim's approach is too lenient."

Tim: "I understand Maureen's concerns, but I think my approach is more about nurturing independence."

Counsellor: "It sounds like you both have valid viewpoints. Let us create a parenting plan that incorporates both structure and freedom."

After the session...

Maureen "I feel like we are finally on the same page. The counsellor's insights were helpful."

Tim: "Absolutely. We now have tools to manage future disagreements more effectively."

Restorative Practice and How It Can Work Through Conflicts

Jocy and Martha have been married for 15 years and in business together for ten years. He is thirty-seven and she is thirty-six years old. They came to therapy because they had been fighting, power struggling, and getting nowhere on their own. This session began with Joey being incredibly angry. The counsellor listened to each of them for a few minutes and then asked them to move into the restorative process, which they had been taught recently.

Counsellor: So, Joey, as you begin, will you tell Martha what the issue is and what feelings this issue generates inside you?

Joey: I am sick of being controlled by you. You want to control my whole life. You leave no area untouched.

Counsellor: You are talking about your wife. I wonder if you could talk about your anger, your hurt, your pain, and what situation results in you feeling controlled.

Joey: You bet I am angry. I am super angry. I did not think marriage would be this way. She tries to control my every move.

Counsellor: Will you tell her about one area where you feel controlled?

Joey: My work. She tells me how to work.

Counsellor: So, you could say, "I feel angry when I believe you are trying to control my work."

Joey: Okay. (Turning to Martha) you are trying to control my work.

Counsellor: And how do you feel?

Joey: It is painful.

Martha: I am not trying to control your work. In fact, all I do is help and give you some ideas.

Counsellor: I know that. But for right now, it is important to uncover a whole picture of what happens, how your husband feels, and what goes on inside him. We would like to know how he ends up feeling angry, believing you are trying to control him, and then fighting with you. Will you ask him to tell you more about how he feels?

Martha: What happens? How do you feel?

Joey: You tell me when to come home from work, how long to spend at work, how to act at work.

Counsellor (to Martha): Will you ask him what that means to him?

Martha: What does that mean to you?

Joey: I just get so, so mad. My life does not belong to me. I am not independent.

Counsellor (to Martha): Ask him to tell you more. In getting the whole picture, you want to know what situations result in him feeling controlled. Also, it seems important to him to feel independent...

Martha: Aren't I asking him to blame me more?

Counsellor: No, it is not about you. It is about his experience of how these events take place between the two of you. In couples, often both people contribute to a painful interaction, but today we are working towards understanding much better how Joey gets so angry with you.

Martha: Okay. When else do you feel controlled?

Joey: About my education. Where and when should I go to work?

Martha: It is not my intention. I like to plan.

Counsellor: I know it is not your intention. This is about Joey's perception. See if you can keep pursuing his image without thinking about yourself and why you do or do not do certain things.

Martha: Where else do you want to be independent?

Joey: In my accounting. You tell me what to charge and it is like you are taking charge of me.

Counsellor: Martha, you are doing an excellent job hanging out with this discussion and trying to learn more about Joey's yearning for independence.

If you are reading this transcript and are not familiar with the restorative process, here are a few headlines about this powerful technique. One aspect of the counselling model is to use the restorative process for effective communication. This process sounds simple but is rich and multi-dimensional.

In the journey of nurturing a strong relationship, couples are introduced to two crucial roles: The Bridger and the Validator. These roles, though seemingly straightforward, are designed to foster deep understanding and effective communication between partners, while providing the therapist with insights into the couple's dynamics.

The Bridger and Validator Roles in Conflict Resolution

Bridger:

- Purpose: Initiate the conversation by addressing a specific issue or problem.

- Approach: Express thoughts and feelings without blaming or name-calling. Stay open to self-discovery.

- Example: Kimmy calmly says, "I feel stressed managing all the cleaning alone. It makes me feel unappreciated." This sets a positive tone for dialogue.

Validator:

- Purpose: Listen actively and reflect on the Bridger's concerns with empathy.

- Approach: Ask questions to understand deeper feelings and respond empathetically.

- Example: Chrysler listens and recaps, "I hear that cleaning alone overwhelms you and makes you feel unappreciated. How does this impact your day?" His empathy helps Kimmy feel heard.

Conflict Resolution Exercise:

1. Define the Issue: Ensure both partners understand the conflict.

2. Cool Down: Take a break if emotions run high.

3. Communicate Openly: Use "I" statements to express feelings without blame.

4. Seek Compromise: Work together to find a solution that satisfies both.

5. Get Help if Needed: Consider a counsellor or mediator if necessary.

By embracing these roles and steps, couples can navigate conflicts with empathy and understanding, strengthening their connection and resilience.

In Short: Bridgers initiate thoughtful conversations about issues, and Validators listen with empathy. Structured conflict resolution can turn conflicts into opportunities for growth.

Reflection

Reflect on the following questions:

- How did resolving the conflict impact on your relationship?

- What strategies worked best for you in resolving the conflict?

- How can you apply these strategies to future disagreements?

Conclusion

Navigating conflict in a relationship is both an art and a science. It requires understanding psychological underpinnings, employing effective communication strategies, and committing to personal and relational growth.

Conflict isn't merely disruptive; it can deepen connection and mutual understanding. Through attachment theory, emotional intelligence, and conflict resolution techniques, couples can turn strife into opportunities for bonding.

Mindful communication, active listening, and seeking support like counselling are key. These methods, alongside activities and self-**reflection, empower couples to navigate conflicts constructively, reinforcing their** partnership.

Ultimately, the journey from strife to strength showcases love's resilience. Embracing conflict as a natural part of relationships enables couples to emerge stronger, equipped to manage future disagreements. Love can indeed conquer all.

References

- Ladd, P. D. (2007). Relationships and patterns of conflict resolution: A reference book for couples counselling. University Press of America.

- Gottman, J. M., & Silver, N. (2015). The seven principles for making marriage work: A practical guide from the country's foremost relationship expert. Harmony Books.

- Markman, H. J., Stanley, S. M., & Blumberg, S. L. (2010). Fighting for your marriage: Positive steps for preventing divorce and preserving a lasting love. Jossey-Bass.

- Fincham, F. D., & Beach, S. R. H. (2010). Conflict in marriage: Implications for working with couples. Annual Review of Psychology, 61(1), 629-651. https://doi.org/10.1146/annurev.psych.093008.100422

- Overall, N. C., & McNulty, J. K. (2017). What type of communication during conflict is beneficial for intimate relationships? Current Opinion in Psychology, 13, 1-5. https://doi.org/10.1016/j.copsyc.2016.03.002

- Tatkin, S. (2012). Wired for love: How understanding your partner's brain and attachment style can help you defuse conflict and build a secure relationship. New Harbinger Publications.

- Grieger, R. (2015). The couple's therapy companion: A cognitive behaviour workbook. Routledge.

- Ratson, M. (2024). Managing conflict resolution effectively. Psychology Today. Retrieved from https://www.psychologytoday.com/us/blog/the-wisdom-of-anger/202401/managing-conflict-resolution-effectively.

- Verywell Health. (2024). Benefits of couples counselling and how it works. Retrieved from https://www.verywellhealth.com/couples-counseling-5205837.

- MAEC, Inc. (2021). Introduction to restorative practices: An equitable approach. Retrieved from https://maec.org/resource/introduction-to-restorative-practices/.

- Bowlby, J. (1988). A Secure Base: Parent-Child Attachment and Healthy Human Development.

Chapter 5

Wanderlust in Harmony: Conversations for Seamless Travel

Planning a holiday together is not just about picking destinations and packing bags; it's a harmonious dance of dreams, compromises, and shared excitement. This chapter guides couples through essential conversations to ensure a smooth, joyous journey. Discover how to align your travel aspirations, balance budgets, and manage expectations, transforming the planning process into an adventure of its own. With each dialogue, you strengthen your bond, setting the stage for an unforgettable escape.

Planning a Holiday Within Our Budget

"Travel is the only thing you buy that makes you richer."-Unknown.

Hand in hand, we dream and plan,

A journey sculpted by love's design.

With stars as our guide and hearts aligned,

We wander the world, leaving worries behind.

Introduction

Planning a holiday within your budget can be both exciting and challenging. It requires careful planning, creativity, and a willingness to prioritize your spending. By setting a budget and sticking to it, you can enjoy a memorable holiday without the stress of overspending. Taking regular holidays is essential for couples as it provides a much-needed break from daily stressors, strengthens the relationship, and enhances overall well-being.

The Importance of Taking Holidays Together

Recharging and Reconnecting: Holidays provide essential opportunities for couples to distress and rejuvenate. They offer a break from the routine and responsibilities, allowing partners to reconnect and deepen their bond. Regular getaways, whether long vacations or short escapes, can significantly enhance relationship satisfaction and individual well-being.

Long and Short Holidays: Balancing long and short holidays within a budget year ensures sustained relaxation and bonding. Long holidays (1-2 weeks) allow for immersive experiences and deep relaxation, while short holidays (weekends or long weekends) offer frequent breaks from daily stressors, keeping the spark alive throughout the year.

Dialogue:

- Sharmila: "Let's plan a long holiday in the summer and a couple of short weekend getaways during the year."

- Brian: "That sounds perfect. We can recharge with a big trip and stay refreshed with mini escapes."

Aligning Travel Aspirations

Discussing Dreams and Desires: At the heart of successful holiday planning lies a shared vision. Couples should openly discuss their ideal holiday scenarios, including destinations, activities, and experiences. This conversation can reveal common interests and highlight areas requiring compromise.

Dialogue:

- Sharmila: "I have always wanted to explore the historical landmarks of Europe."

- Brian: "That sounds amazing! I am drawn to the beaches in Southeast Asia. Can we find a way to incorporate both?"

Budgeting Together

Financial Transparency and Planning: Openly discussing finances is crucial. Couples should agree on a budget that aligns with their financial situation and travel goals. This includes saving strategies, expenditure limits, and contingency plans.

Strategies for Effective Budgeting:

- Create a joint travel fund.

- Prioritize expenses (accommodation, experiences, meals).

- Use budgeting apps to track spending in real time.

Dialogue:

- Brian: " We need to set a realistic budget. How much can we comfortably allocate for this trip?"

- Sharmila: "I agree. Let us also factor in some extra for unexpected expenses."

Affordable and Inexpensive Holidays

Travel on a Budget: Holidays do not need to break the bank. There are numerous budget-friendly options that still offer fulfilling experiences. Camping, road trips and staycations can be incredibly rejuvenated without incurring significant costs.

Budget-Friendly Destinations:

- Camping: Embrace nature and enjoy a budget-friendly escape by camping in national parks or local campgrounds.

- Road Trips: Explore nearby towns and scenic routes. Pack meals and stay in affordable accommodations like motels or hostels.

- Staycations: Transform your home into a retreat. Plan day trips, dine out at local restaurants, and take advantage of nearby attractions.

Dialogue:

- Sean: "We can save money by camping for our next trip. It's affordable and we get to enjoy nature."

- Julianna:: "I love that idea! Let us find a beautiful spot and plan some activities like hiking and stargazing."

Managing Expectations

Defining Roles and Responsibilities: Dividing tasks can streamline the planning process and play to each partner's strengths. This includes research, booking accommodations, itinerary planning, and packing.

Example Dialogue:

Sean: "I will oversee booking the flights and accommodations."
Julianna: "Perfect, I'll research activities and dining options."

Compromise and Flexibility

Balancing Preferences: Compromise is essential in holiday planning. Couples should be willing to adapt and adjust to accommodate each other's preferences.

Dialogue:

- Ana:: "I really want to spend a day at the museum."

- Herbert: "Sure, and maybe we can dedicate the next day to outdoor adventures?"

Practical Activities and Tools

Activity: Travel Wishlist: Create a shared travel wish list where each partner lists their top destinations and activities. Compare and prioritize finding common ground and create a balanced itinerary.

Exercise: Budget Planning Workshop: Set aside time to sit together and plan the budget. Use online tools and resources to estimate costs and track savings.

Tool: Itinerary Planner: Utilize digital itinerary planners like Google Trips or TripIt to organize travel plans, share with each other, and ensure nothing is overlooked.

Self-Reflection Practices

Journaling: Encourage each partner to maintain a travel journal. Documenting experiences, thoughts, and emotions can enhance the travel experience and provide a meaningful keepsake.

Mindfulness: Practice mindfulness during the trip to stay present and appreciate each moment. Techniques like deep breathing, meditation, and mindful walking can help couples fully engage with their surroundings and each other.

Journaling: Encourage each partner to maintain a travel journal. Documenting experiences, thoughts, and emotions can enhance the travel experience and provide a meaningful keepsake.

Mindfulness: Practice mindfulness during the trip to stay present and appreciate each moment. Techniques like deep breathing, meditation, and mindful walking can help couples fully engage with their surroundings and each other.

Examples of Conversations

1. **Yvone and Andrew** wanted to take a family vacation but were concerned about the costs. They decided to plan a budget-friendly trip by choosing a nearby destination, booking accommodation in advance, and looking for free or low-cost activities. They also decided to take some vacations in a rented caravan. This approach allowed them to have a fun and affordable holiday.

2. **Maryann and Laz:** Maryann and Laz set a goal to save for their dream vacation. They created a savings plan, cut back on non-essential expenses, and used travel rewards points to reduce costs. Their careful planning paid off, and they were able to enjoy a fantastic holiday without financial strain.

Maryann: "Laz, I really want to take a vacation, but I'm worried about how much it will cost."

Laz: "I understand, Maryann. Let us set a budget and see how we can make it work. We can start by choosing a destination that is close by to save on travel expenses."

Maryann: "That is a clever idea. We can also look for deals on accommodations and plan some free activities."

Laz: "Agreed. Let us make a list of all the expenses and see where we can cut costs. We can still have a wonderful time without spending a fortune."

Activity: Creating a Holiday Budget

Step 1: Set Your Budget

- Determine how much you can afford to spend on your holiday. Consider all sources of income and any savings you can allocate for the trip.

Step 2: List of All Expenses

- Make a list of all potential expenses, including travel, accommodation, food, activities, and souvenirs.

Step 3: Prioritize Spending

- Decide which expenses are most important to you and allocate your budget accordingly. Look for ways to save, such as booking in advance, using discounts, and choosing budget-friendly options.

Step 4: Track Your Spending

- Keep track of your expenses before and during the trip to ensure you stay within your budget. Use a budgeting app or a simple spreadsheet to monitor your spending.

Reflection

Reflect on the following questions:

- How did setting a budget help you plan your holiday?

- What strategies did you use to stay within your budget?

- How can you apply these budgeting skills to other areas of your life?

Conclusion

Embracing the Journey: Holiday planning is a unique opportunity for couples to collaborate, dream, and strengthen their bond. By engaging in open conversations, practicing effective budgeting, and embracing compromise, couples can ensure their travels are not only seamless but also enriching. This harmonious approach transforms the planning process into an extension of the holiday itself, fostering deeper connection and lasting memories.

References

- Bodenmann, G. (1997). Dyadic coping - a systemic-transactional view of stress and coping among couples: Theory and empirical findings. European Review of Applied Psychology, 47(2), 137-140.

- Bühler, J. L., Krauss, S., & Orth, U. (2021). Development of relationship satisfaction across the life span: A systematic review and meta-analysis. Psychological Bulletin, 147(10), 1012–1053. https://doi.org/10.1037/bul0000342

- Lau, K. K. H., Randall, A. K., Duran, N. D., & Tao, C. (2019). Examining the effects of couples' real-time stress and coping processes on interaction quality: Language use as a mediator. Frontiers in Psychology, 9, 2598. https://doi.org/10.3389/fpsyg.2018.02598

- Myers-Walls, J. A., & Futris, T. (2020). Rituals and couples: Understanding the role of rituals in relationship stage transitions. Family Focus, Spring 2020, 1-18. Retrieved from https://www.ncfr.org/system/files/2020-04/Focus%20%20Spring%202020.pdf.

- Randall, A. K., & Bodenmann, G. (2009). The role of stress on close relationships and marital satisfaction. Clinical Psychology Review, 29(2), 105-115. https://doi.org/10.1016/j.cpr.2008.10.004

Chapter 6

Mastering Your Connections: Speaking Each Other's Love Language

The concept of love languages revolutionizes how couples communicate and connect. This chapter explores the five love languages—words of affirmation, acts of service, receiving gifts, quality time, and physical touch and how understanding and speaking these languages can deepen your relationship. By recognizing and responding to your partner's love language, you can foster greater intimacy, satisfaction, and emotional security. Discover practical strategies and exercises to master this vital aspect of relational harmony.

"Your love language resonates with those who truly listen and respond kindly. Embrace it and take the time to understand theirs as well."

In the dance of love, understanding your partner's rhythm creates harmony." Valerie Monteiro

In the symphony of love, our hearts compose,

Each word, each touch, in harmony it flows.

Through acts and time, gifts and praise, we

see, A love enriched, in languages set free.

Introduction:

Understanding and speaking each other's love language is fundamental to deepening intimacy and fostering a lasting connection. Dr. Gary Chapman's pioneering work on love languages reveals that each person expresses and experiences love in unique ways. By identifying and embracing these languages, couples can bridge gaps in communication, meet each other's emotional needs more effectively, and cultivate a relationship that thrives on mutual understanding and affection.

In this chapter, we delve into the five primary love languages and offer practical insights and activities to help you, and your partner become fluent in each other's emotional dialect. Whether you are newly together or have spent decades side by side, mastering the art of love languages can transform your bond, ensuring that love is not only felt but also profoundly understood and reciprocated.

The Five Love Languages:

1. **Words of Affirmation:**

    o   Expressing love through spoken or written words of praise, appreciation, and encouragement. Simple statements like "I love you," "You mean the world to me," or "I appreciate everything you do" can make a significant impact.

2. **Quality Time:**

    o   Giving your partner undivided attention. This means engaging in meaningful conversations, sharing activities, and being fully present. It is about making time to connect without distractions.

3. **Physical Touch:**

    o   Showing love through physical contact such as hugging, kissing, holding hands, and other forms of affectionate touch. This love language emphasises the importance of physical closeness and intimacy.

4. **Acts of Service:**

    o   Demonstrating love by doing things that help or support your partner. This could be anything from cooking a meal, doing household chores, or running errands. It's about easing your partner's burdens.

5. **Receiving Gifts:**

    o   Expressing love through thoughtful gifts that show you were thinking about your partner. These gifts don't have to be expensive; it's the thought and effort that count.

Understanding Different Needs: Couples often have different primary love languages, which can lead to misunderstandings and frustration. For example, one partner might feel unloved because they value quality time, while the other expresses love through acts of service. Recognizing and respecting these differences is crucial for a harmonious relationship.

Addressing Different Sex Drives and Idiosyncrasies: Sexual compatibility is another important aspect of relationships. Partners may have different sex drives, preferences, and styles, which can lead to frustration if not addressed openly. It is essential to communicate your needs and be willing to compromise. Understanding that these differences are normal and finding ways to meet each other's needs can strengthen your bond.

Take a few minutes to complete the Love Language Quiz. You can find the quiz online or use the following questions to guide you:

1. How do you feel most loved by your partner?
   - A. When they give you a hug or kiss.
   - B. When they spend quality time with you.
   - C. When they do something helpful for you.
   - D. When they give you a thoughtful gift.
   - E. When they say kind and affirming words to you.

2. What do you most often request from your partner?
   - A. Physical affection.
   - B. Time together.
   - C. Help with tasks.
   - D. Gifts or surprises.
   - E. Compliments or words of encouragement.

3. How do you usually express love to your partner?
   - A. Through physical touch.
   - B. By spending time together.
   - C. By doing things for them.
   - D. By giving gifts.
   - E. By speaking kind words.

Exploring practical strategies to learn each other's love language can significantly strengthen a relationship. Imagine Malcolm and Marietta, a couple eager to understand and express their love more profoundly. They embark on this journey with curiosity and dedication.

Taking the Love Languages Quiz

One evening, **Marietta suggests, "Malcolm**, let's take the love languages quiz on Dr. Gary Chapman's website to identify our primary love languages." Intrigued, Malcolm agrees. They sit together, each answering questions about how they feel loved and appreciated. The quiz reveals that Marietta's primary love language is Acts of Service, while Malcolm's is Quality Time.

Sharing and Discussing Results

The next step involves sharing their results. Malcolm starts, "Marietta, I feel most loved when we spend time together without distractions. What about you?" Marietta responds, "I feel appreciated when you help around the house or do something thoughtful for me." This discussion helps them understand how to incorporate each other's love languages into their daily lives.

Practicing Regularly

They make a conscious effort to speak each other's love language daily. Malcolm begins leaving little love notes for Marietta, while she surprises him by planning regular date nights. They also find small ways to express their love, such as Malcolm doing the dishes without being asked, and Marietta dedicating time each evening for deep conversations.

Reflecting and Adjusting

Periodically, they check in with each other to see how well they're meeting each other's needs. During one of these check-ins, Malcolm asks, "Marietta, how do you feel about the time we're spending together?" Marietta appreciates his effort and offers feedback, "I love our dates, but maybe we can add some new activities we both enjoy."

Celebrating Progress

They make it a point to celebrate their progress. Acknowledging and appreciating each other's efforts reinforces positive behaviour and strengthens their connection. On their anniversary, Marietta says, "Malcolm, I've really felt the difference in how we express our love. Thank you for being so thoughtful."

Conversation 1: Discovering Love Languages

Cheryl and Agnel sit down for a heart-to-heart. Cheryl begins, "Agnel, I've been reading about love languages, and I think it could help us understand each other better. Do you know what your love language is?"

Agnel replies, "I've heard about them, but I'm not sure. What are they again?"

Cheryl explains, "There are five: Words of Affirmation, Quality Time, Physical Touch, Acts of Service, and Receiving Gifts. Mine is Quality Time. I feel most loved when we spend time together without distractions."

Agnel nods, "That makes sense. I think mine might be Words of Affirmation. I feel appreciated when you validate me or encourage me when I have done something thoughtful for you. "

Cheryl smiles, "That's good to know. Let's try to express our love in ways that resonate with each other."

Conversation 2: Addressing Different Sex Drives

Kevin and Adrianna face a sensitive issue with care.

Kevin starts, "Adrianna, I've noticed that we have different sex drives, and it's been causing some tension. Can we talk about it?"

Adrianna acknowledges, "I've noticed that too, Kevin. It has been on my mind. We need to find a balance that works for both of us. It's really difficult with my shifts and timings and tending to the needs of the children and I do want to connect."

Kevin suggests, "Maybe we can set aside specific times for intimacy and find other ways to connect physically, like cuddling or holding hands."

Adrianna agrees, "That sounds like a good plan. I want us both to feel satisfied and connected."

Self-Reflections

Malcolm and Marietta engage in self-reflection to deepen their understanding:

Personal Love Language: Marietta reflects on how Acts of Service make her feel loved and appreciated. She realizes that undivided attention from Malcolm strengthens her emotional bond.

Partner's Love Language: Malcolm considers how Quality Time resonates with him and thinks about how he can better express his love in ways that resonate with Marietta.

Sexual Compatibility: They reflect on their sexual needs and preferences, discussing how they can communicate these to each other to foster understanding and compromise.

Academic Perspectives

While Chapman's love languages have gained widespread popularity, empirical research on their effectiveness is limited. A study by Impett et al. (2024) highlights that the concept of love languages resonates with people because it helps identify important relationship needs and offers a straightforward way to improve relationships. However, the study notes a lack of strong empirical support for the idea that matching love languages directly correlates with relationship satisfaction. Another study by Mostova et al. (2022) found that partners who respond to each other's love language preferences experience greater relationship and sexual satisfaction, emphasizing the importance of empathy in understanding and meeting a partner's needs.

Practical Strategies

1. Identify Your Love Languages: Couples should take the time to understand their own and their partner's preferred love languages. This can be done through self-reflection and open communication.

2. Communicate Openly: Discussing love languages can help partners express their needs and preferences more clearly. This can lead to a deeper understanding and stronger emotional connection.

3. Practice Empathy: Empathy plays a crucial role in responding to a partner's love language. Being attuned to each other's emotional needs can enhance relationship satisfaction.

4. Be Flexible: While it is important to recognize and honour each other's love languages, couples should also be open to adapting and trying new ways of expressing love.

Conclusion

Learning each other's love languages is a powerful tool for enhancing intimacy and connection in a relationship. By understanding and practicing these languages, couples can ensure that both partners feel valued and loved. Open communication about sexual needs and preferences is also crucial for maintaining a healthy and satisfying relationship. Remember, love is an ongoing process that requires effort, understanding, and a willingness to grow together.

References

Chapman, G. D. (1995). The five love languages: How to express heartfelt commitment to your mate. Chicago: Northfield Pub2

Impett, E. A., Park, H. G., & Muise, A. (2024). Popular psychology through a scientific lens: Evaluating love languages from a relationship science perspective3.

Current Directions in Psychological Science, 33(2), 87-923

Mostova, O., Stolarski, M., & Matthews, G. (2022). I love the way you love me: Responding to partner's love language preferences boosts satisfaction in romantic heterosexual couples. PLOS ONE, 17(6), e0269429

Chapter 7

Crafting Your Legacy: Creating Family Traditions and Rituals

Family traditions and rituals form the bedrock of a shared history, instilling a sense of belonging and continuity. This chapter explores the importance of creating and sustaining unique family traditions that reflect your values, culture, and interests. Learn how to design meaningful rituals that foster connections across generations, celebrate milestones, and enhance everyday life. Whether it's holiday customs, weekly routines, or special celebrations, these practices will enrich your family narrative and strengthen your bonds.

"Family traditions are the glue that binds us together, the legacy we pass on, and the joy we share across generations."

In the tapestry of time, our stories we weave,
Threads of joy and love, in rituals we believe.
From morning songs to festive nights,
Family traditions shine their light.

Introduction

Creating family traditions and rituals is an essential aspect of nurturing a sense of identity and continuity. These practices offer moments of connection and celebration, providing a framework within which family members can express love, share value, and build memories. In an ever-changing world, these enduring customs create a stable foundation, offering comfort and a sense of belonging.

This chapter delves into the significance of family traditions, offering insights into how to craft meaningful rituals that resonate with your family's unique dynamics.

From establishing new holiday traditions to incorporating daily rituals, we will explore the profound impact these practices have on individual well-being and familial unity.

Family traditions are the bedrock of a strong and connected household, offering numerous benefits that span emotional, cultural, and psychological realms. These rituals help build connection and continuity by providing regular opportunities for family members to bond. Through shared practices and values, they foster a sense of belonging and identity, linking generations in a meaningful way.

Take the **Johnson family,** for instance. Every Sunday evening, they gather for a family dinner where everyone pitches in to cook. This tradition not only allows them to enjoy a delicious meal together but also provides a regular opportunity to connect and share their week's experiences. It is a time for laughter, storytelling, and building deeper relationships.

Traditions also play a crucial role in preserving cultural heritage and personal history. They serve as a tangible link to the past, allowing families to celebrate their legacies and reinforce a sense of pride and identity. For example, the **Garcia family** celebrates Dia de los Muertos each year, honouring their ancestors with a beautiful altar and stories passed down through generations. This annual celebration reinforces their cultural roots and brings the family together in remembrance and gratitude.

Moreover, regular rituals provide significant emotional and psychological benefits. The stability and predictability that come with traditions are essential for emotional well-being, offering comfort during times of change and stress. They create a safe space where family members can express their feelings and support one another, fostering a nurturing environment. The Smiths, for example, have a tradition of Friday movie nights. No matter how hectic the week gets, they know they can unwind together, creating a sense of security and togetherness.

Creating and sustaining these traditions begins with identifying the core values and interests that define your family. Whether it is a love for the outdoors, a passion for cooking, or a commitment to community service, these can form the foundation of meaningful family traditions. The Nguyen family, enthusiastic about the outdoors, has an annual camping trip where they explore new trails and enjoy nature. This shared adventure not only strengthens their bond but also instils a love for nature in their children.

In essence, family traditions are more than just routines; they are powerful tools for building a cohesive, supportive, and loving family unit. By embracing and nurturing these traditions, families can create a rich tapestry of shared experiences and memories that strengthen their bonds and enrich their lives. For instance, the Ahmed family, committed to community service, spends one Saturday a month volunteering together at a local shelter. This tradition teaches their children the value of giving back and reinforces their family's commitment to helping others.

By incorporating these examples, we can see how family traditions uniquely shape and strengthen the fabric of family life, providing a foundation of love, support, and shared identity that endures through generations.

Dialogue:

- Daniel: "We both love nature and hiking. How about we start an annual family hiking trip?"

- Tessie: "That sounds perfect. We can explore a new trail every year and make it a fun family adventure."

Start Small and Build: Introduce new traditions gradually. Start with simple, manageable activities and expand them over time. Consistency is key, so choose rituals that fit naturally into your family's routine.

Dialogue:

- Juliet: "Let us start a weekly game night every Friday and a prayer circle on Sunday afternoons. I would really like our family to have fun when we meet and also keep the tradition of faith in our lives."

- Glenn: "I love that idea! We can take turns choosing the game and also in choosing the prayer passages."

Incorporate Milestones and Celebrations: Create traditions around significant milestones and celebrations. Birthdays, holidays, and anniversaries offer perfect opportunities to establish meaningful rituals.

Example Dialogue:

- Derek: "For our anniversary, let's write letters to each other reflecting on the past year."

- Karen: "Beautiful idea. We can read them aloud over a special dinner."

Practical Activities and Rituals

Daily and Weekly Rituals:

- Morning Rituals: Begin the day with a family breakfast or a short walk together.
- Weekly Rituals: Establish a family movie night or a Sunday roast tradition.

Seasonal and Annual Traditions:

- Holiday Customs: Create unique holiday traditions, such as crafting decorations together or baking family recipes.
- Annual Events: Plan yearly family reunions or trips to a favourite location.

Special Celebrations:

- Birthdays: Develop birthday rituals like a special breakfast in bed or a family talent show.
- Milestones: Celebrate achievements with personalized ceremonies or memory books.

The Power of Compliments: Add these to your daily rituals:

Compliments are a simple yet powerful way to make your partner feel valued and loved. They can boost self-esteem and reinforce positive behaviours. Here are some tips for giving meaningful compliments:

- **Be Specific:** Instead of saying, "You look nice," try "I love how that dress brings out the colour of your eyes."
- **Be Genuine:** Only give compliments that you truly mean. Authenticity is key.
- **Focus on Effort:** Acknowledge the effort your partner puts into something, like "I appreciate how hard you worked on that project."

Appreciating Your Partner

Appreciation goes beyond compliments. It's about recognizing and valuing your partner's contributions to the relationship and your life together. Here are some ways to show appreciation:

- **Express Gratitude:** Regularly thank your partner for the little things they do, like making coffee or taking out the trash.

- **Write a Note:** Leave a heartfelt note for your partner to find, expressing your appreciation for something specific they did.

- **Acts of Kindness:** Show appreciation through small acts of kindness, like cooking their favourite meal or giving them a massage.

Expressing Feelings

Openly expressing your feelings can deepen your connection and foster intimacy. Here are some strategies for sharing your emotions:

- **Use "I" Statements:** Frame your feelings with "I" statements to avoid sounding accusatory. For example, "I feel loved when you hold my hand."

- **Be Vulnerable:** Share your fears, hopes, and dreams with your partner. Vulnerability can strengthen your bond.

- **Listen Actively:** When your partner expresses their feelings, listen without interrupting and show empathy.

Activities to Foster These Conversations

1. **Compliment Jar:** Create a jar where you and your partner can drop in compliments for each other. Read them together at the end of the week.

2. **Appreciation Journal:** Keep a journal where you both write down things you appreciate about each other daily.

3. **Feelings Check-In:** Set aside time each week to check in with each other about your feelings and discuss any concerns or joys.

By incorporating these conversations into your relationship, you can create a more loving, appreciative, and emotionally connected partnership. Remember, it's never too late to start having the conversations. In "Conscious Conversations for Committed Couples," we have explored the importance of open, honest, and meaningful communication in building and maintaining strong, healthy relationships.

By engaging in conscious conversations, couples can deepen their understanding of each other, resolve conflicts more effectively, and create a shared vision for their future. The activities and reflections included in this book are designed to foster connection, empathy, and mutual respect, helping couples navigate the complexities of their relationship with greater ease and confidence.

Remember, the journey of a committed relationship is an ongoing process that requires continuous effort, patience, and love. By prioritizing conscious conversations, couples can strengthen their bond, enhance their emotional intimacy, and build a lasting partnership based on trust and mutual support.

Self-Reflection Practices

Journaling: Encourage family members to document their experiences and feelings about the traditions. Journaling can enhance the sense of connection and provide a cherished family history record.

Mindfulness: Practice mindfulness during family rituals to fully engage and appreciate the moments spent together. Techniques like deep breathing and reflective discussion can enrich the experience.

Conclusion:

Creating and sustaining family traditions and rituals are powerful ways to build lasting connections, celebrate shared values, and foster a sense of belonging. These practices not only enhance individual well-being but also strengthen the familial bond, providing a source of joy and stability. By crafting your own unique traditions, you can leave a legacy of love and connection that will be cherished for generations to come.

1. Sillars, A. L., & Vangelisti, A. L. (2018). Communication: Basic properties and their relevance to relationship research. In A. L. Vangelisti & D. Perlman (Eds.), The Cambridge handbook of personal relationships (2nd ed., pp. 243–255). Cambridge University Press. https://doi.org/10.1017/9781316417867.020

2. Frahm, W. A. (2010). Long-distance romantic relationships: Connections among conflict, uncertainty, maintenance, and mediated communication use (master's thesis, North Dakota University). Retrieved from https://library.ndsu.edu/ir/bitstream/handle/10365/33735/Frahm%2c%20 Whitney%20Allison_Communication%20MA_2010.pdf?sequence=1.

3. Paynton, S. T., & Hahn, L. K. (n.d.). Interpersonal communication references. In Introduction to Communication. Humboldt State University. Retrieved from https://socialsci.libretexts.org/Bookshelves/Communication/Introduction_t o_Communication/Introduction_to_Communication_%28Paynton_and_Ha hn%29/09/09%3A_Interpersonal_Communication/9.09%3A_Interpersonal_Co mmunication_References.

Module 3
The Journey of Parenthood:
Common Issues and Fixes

Chapter 1

Balancing Love and Parenthood: Bringing Baby Home

Welcoming a new baby is one of the most profound changes a couple can experience. This chapter explores how to navigate the transition from couple-hood to parenthood without losing the essence of your partnership. Learn strategies to balance the joys and challenges of parenthood, maintain a strong connection with your partner, and create a nurturing environment for your newborn. Couples can strengthen their bond and build a resilient family foundation by embracing this transformative journey together.

"The greatest joy is not only in bringing a new life into the world but in nurturing the life you've built together."

In the gentle hush of dawn, a baby's cry we hear

Two hearts beat stronger, united in love and cheer

From couple to parents, our journey unfolds,

A dance of love and life as new stories are told.

Introduction

The arrival of children brings immense joy and fulfilment, but it also introduces new challenges for couples. Balancing the demands of parenthood while maintaining a strong, loving relationship requires effort, communication, and intentionality. By prioritizing your relationship and finding ways to connect amidst the chaos, you can continue to nurture your bond as a couple.

Bringing a baby home is a monumental milestone filled with excitement, joy, and a fair share of challenges. This transition from being a couple to becoming parents can evaluate your relationship's strength while offering opportunities for profound growth and deeper connection. The early days of parenthood are a delicate balancing function as you navigate sleepless nights, new responsibilities, and the overwhelming love for your newborn.

In this chapter, we delve into the intricacies of maintaining your relationship amidst the demands of parenting. We will explore strategies for sustaining intimacy, effective communication, and shared responsibilities. By prioritizing your partnership alongside parenthood, you can create a harmonious and loving environment for both your child and you.

The Journey of Parenthood: Common Issues and Fixes

When Leo and Joanna welcomed their first child, their hearts were filled with joy and excitement. Little did they know that the journey of parenthood would be filled with a myriad of challenges that would test their patience, resilience, and love.

Sleep Deprivation

One of the first hurdles they encountered was sleep deprivation. Their newborn, Lily, had a knack for waking up every two hours during the night. "I feel like a zombie," Joanna confessed one morning. To combat this, they tried different sleep strategies, such as swaddling, white noise machines, and establishing a bedtime routine. They also took turns for night shifts, allowing each other to get some much-needed rest. Over time, they found a rhythm that worked for their family.

Feeding Challenges

Feeding was another significant challenge. Joanna struggled with breastfeeding, feeling guilty for not producing enough milk. "It's okay to supplement with formula," Leo reassured her. They consulted a lactation specialist who provided guidance and support, and eventually, they found a feeding routine that ensured Lily was well-nourished and healthy.

Balancing Work and Family

As working parents, Leo and Joanna found it difficult to balance their careers and family life. "I feel like I'm not giving my best at work or at home," Leo admitted. They decided to set clear boundaries, such as designated family time in the evenings and no work emails after 7 PM. They also enlisted the help of family members for childcare, allowing them to focus on their jobs without feeling overwhelmed.

Handling Tantrums

As Lily grew older, tantrums became a part of their daily life. "Why does she get so upset over the smallest things?" Joanna wondered. They learned that tantrums are a normal part of toddler development and started using positive reinforcement techniques, such as praising good behaviour and offering choices to give Lily a sense of control. This approach helped reduce the frequency and intensity of tantrums.

Sibling Rivalry

When their second child, Archie, was born, sibling rivalry emerged. "Lily seems so jealous of Archie," Leo noticed. They made a conscious effort to spend quality time with Lily, reassuring her of their love. They also involved her in caring for Archie, making her feel like an important part of the family. Over time, Lily began to embrace her role as an older sister.

Parental Self-Care

Amidst all these challenges, Leo and Joanna realized the importance of self-care. "We need to take care of ourselves to be the best parents we can be," Joanna said. They scheduled regular date nights and engaged in hobbies they enjoyed, whether it was reading, exercising, or simply taking a quiet walk together. This time for themselves helped them recharge and stay connected.

Discipline and Boundaries

Establishing discipline and boundaries was crucial as their children grew older. "Consistency is key," Leo emphasized. They created a set of house rules and consequences, ensuring that both Lily and Archie understood them. They used time-outs and loss of privileges as discipline methods, always reinforcing the lessons with love and patience.

Communication and Support

Throughout their journey, open communication and support were vital. Leo and Joanna made it a point to discuss their feelings and concerns regularly. "We need to be a team," Leo reminded Joanna. They also sought advice from parenting books, online resources, and support groups, finding comfort in knowing they were not alone.

Conclusion

The journey of parenthood is filled with both joys and challenges. Leo and Joanna learned that facing these challenges together, with patience, understanding, and a willingness to seek help, made them stronger as individuals and as a family. By addressing common parenting issues with practical solutions, they created a nurturing and supportive environment for their children to thrive.

As they continue their journey, Leo and Joanna remain committed to navigating the difficulties of parenthood, knowing that each challenge they overcome brings them closer together and makes their family bond even stronger.

The Transition from Couple to Parents: Transitioning from a couple to parents involves significant changes in dynamics, roles, and responsibilities. This shift can strain even the strongest relationships as partners navigate new identities and expectations. Research indicates that new parents often experience declines in marital satisfaction due to increased stress, sleep deprivation, and time constraints.

Key Challenges:

1. **Sleep Deprivation:** The relentless demands of a newborn can lead to chronic sleep deprivation, which negatively impacts mood, patience, and the ability to communicate effectively. In the earlier times, parenting in most cultures was a huge event, where couples had help from parents and elders and other relatives. However, with nuclear families, most couples must adjust to working and looking after a baby which is like a full-time job.

2. **Division of Labour:** Balancing household and childcare duties can become a point of contention. Traditional gender roles may resurface, leading to perceived inequities and resentment, and this can be avoided.

3. **Maintaining Intimacy:** Physical and emotional intimacy often takes a backseat as couples focus on their baby and are usually tired and overworked. Finding time and energy for each other becomes challenging; however, enlisting support from family and friends can go a long way.

4. Communication Breakdown: The stress and exhaustion of new parenthood can hamper effective communication, leading to misunderstandings and conflicts. Watch out for the signs of arguments and fights.

Balancing Love and Parenthood: Bringing Baby Home

When Samantha and Nathan welcomed their newborn daughter, Ava-Lily, their world transformed overnight. The transition from being a couple to becoming parents brought significant changes in their dynamics, roles, and responsibilities. Even the strongest relationships can be assessed during this time, as partners navigate new identities and expectations. Research suggests that new parents often experience declines in marital satisfaction due to increased stress, sleep deprivation, and time constraints (Lawrence et al., 2008).

Key Challenges

One of the most immediate challenges Nathan and Samantha faced was sleep deprivation. The relentless demands of caring for a newborn led to chronic sleep loss, impacting their mood, patience, and ability to communicate effectively. Mornings turned into hazy, sleep-deprived negotiations about who would take the next shift.

Balancing household and childcare duties soon became another point of contention. Traditional gender roles resurfaced, leading to perceived inequities and resentment. Samantha felt overwhelmed managing both the baby and the household chores, while Nathan struggled to find a balance between work and his new responsibilities at home.

Maintaining intimacy also became difficult. Physical and emotional closeness took a backseat as they focused on their baby. Finding the time and energy for each other amidst the chaos of parenthood was a challenge. The stress and exhaustion led to communication breakdowns, with misunderstandings and conflicts arising more frequently.

The Importance of Maintaining a Strong Relationship After Becoming Parents

Samantha and Nathan realized that maintaining a strong relationship was crucial for their family's well-being. A solid partnership forms the cornerstone of a healthy family dynamic. When partners prioritize their connection, they model a loving and supportive relationship for their child, providing a secure environment where Ava-lily can thrive emotionally and developmentally.

Navigating the challenges of parenthood requires emotional resilience. Their relationship became a source of support and strength, helping them cope with stress, adapt to changes, and maintain a positive outlook. When they felt connected, they were better equipped to manage the demands of raising Ava-Lily.

Sharing the joys and challenges of parenthood with a loving partner deepened their sense of accomplishment and happiness. Celebrating milestones like Ava-Lily's first smile or overcoming obstacles together strengthened their emotional bond.

A harmonious relationship also fostered effective co-parenting. Open communication and collaboration allowed Samantha and Nathan to make unified decisions regarding Ava-Lily's upbringing. This consistency provided Ava-Lily with clear guidance and reinforced her sense of security.

Maintaining a strong relationship also allowed Samantha and Nathan to continue growing as individuals. Supporting each other's personal goals and interests outside of parenthood ensured that both felt valued and fulfilled, preventing feelings of resentment, and fostering mutual respect.

Practical Strategies for Maintaining Your Relationship

To keep their relationship strong, Samantha and Nathan adopted several practical strategies. They made it a priority to set aside quality time for each other, even if it was just a few minutes each day. They enjoyed daily walks with Ava-Lily, weekly date nights, and quiet moments together after she was asleep.

They maintained open lines of communication, sharing their thoughts, feelings, and concerns honestly, and listening to each other with empathy and understanding. Expressing gratitude for each other's contributions and efforts, no matter how small, went a long way in reinforcing a positive and supportive environment.

They sought support from family and friends, understanding that a staunch support network could alleviate some of the pressures of parenthood, allowing them to focus on their relationship. Keeping the physical connection alive through hugs, kisses, and other forms of affection helped maintain intimacy and reinforced their emotional bonds.

Finally, they encouraged each other to take time for self-care. By prioritizing their well-being, they could bring their best selves to the relationship and parenthood.

Through these strategies, Emma and Jake found that they could balance love and parenthood, ensuring their relationship remained strong and their family dynamic, healthy and happy.

Practical Strategies for Maintaining Your Relationship

Prioritize Quality Time: Regularly set aside time for each other, even if it's just a few minutes each day. This could be a daily walk, a weekly date night, or a quiet moment together after the baby is asleep.

Communicate Openly: Maintain open lines of communication. Share your thoughts, feelings, and concerns honestly, and listen to each other with empathy and understanding.

Show Appreciation: Express gratitude for each other's contributions and efforts. Small gestures of appreciation go a long way in reinforcing a positive and supportive environment.

Seek Support: Do not hesitate to seek help from family, friends, or professional resources. Having a dedicated support network can alleviate some of the pressures of parenthood, allowing you to focus on your relationship.

Maintain Physical Affection: Keep the physical connection alive through hugs, kisses, and other forms of affection. Physical touch helps maintain intimacy and reinforces emotional bonds.

Practice Self-Care: Encourage each other to take time for self-care. When both partners prioritize their well-being, they can bring their best selves to the relationship and parenthood.

Reflective Activity

Relationship Check-In: Schedule regular relationship check-ins to discuss how you're feeling, and any adjustments needed. Use this time to reflect on your relationship's strengths and areas for improvement.

Example Reflection Questions:

How do I feel about our relationship since becoming parents?

What are some recent successes we have had in supporting each other?

What adjustments can we make to improve our connection?

Conversations

Andrea: "Allen, I miss spending time with you. I feel like we are always focused on the baby and never on us."

Allen: "I feel the same way, babes. How about setting aside one night a week for just us? We can have dinner together after the baby is asleep."

Andrea: "That sounds perfect. We can also ask our parents to babysit occasionally so we can go out for a walk or a movie."

Allen: "Agreed. Let us make it a priority to have our time together."

Andrea and Allen found it challenging to spend quality time together after their baby was born. They decided to schedule regular date nights, even if it meant just having a quiet dinner at home after the baby was asleep. This helped them reconnect and maintain their bond. They even got their elder son Aiden to baby sit during their dinner times, so they could catch up on the day's events.

Harvey and Shirley: Harvey and Shirley struggled with balancing their roles as parents and partners. Ever since the twins came along. They needed to enlist the help of both sets of parents, who lovingly gave them their time. They started a weekly tradition of taking a walk together while their parents babysat. This simple routine allowed them to have uninterrupted time to talk and enjoy each other's company.

Activity: Creating Couple Time

Step 1: Identify Opportunities for Connection

- List activities you both enjoy and can do together, such as cooking, watching a movie, or taking a walk.

Step 2: Schedule Regular Date Nights

- Set a specific day and time each week for a date night. It does not have to be elaborate; the key is to spend quality time together.

Step 3: Utilize Support Systems

- Ask family or friends to babysit occasionally to give you some alone time. Do not hesitate to seek help when needed.

Step 4: Communicate Openly

- Discuss your needs and feelings with your partner. Make sure you both feel heard and supported.

Reflection

Reflect on the following questions:

- How did setting aside a couple of times impact your relationship?
- What activities did you enjoy the most together?
- How can you continue to prioritize your relationship amidst the demands of parenthood?
- What were our biggest challenges this week?
- How did we support each other effectively?
- What can we do differently next week to improve our partnership?

Practical Strategies

Effective Communication: Prioritize open and honest communication to navigate the complexities of new parenthood. Use "I" statements to express feelings without blame, and practice active listening.

Dialogue:

- Tina: "I feel overwhelmed with the nighttime feedings. Can we discuss how to share this responsibility?"

- Roy: "I understand. Let us find a way to alternate nights, so we both get some rest."

Shared Responsibilities: Equitably distribute household and childcare tasks to prevent burnout and resentment. Regularly reassess and adjust responsibilities based on each partner's capacity.

Dialogue:

- Theresa: "I am finding it hard to keep up with the cooking. Can you take on dinner prep for a while?"

- Brodie: "Absolutely, I will manage dinners. Let us make a meal plan together."

Maintaining Intimacy: Schedule regular date nights, even if it is just a short walk or a movie at home. Physical affection, such as holding hands or cuddling, helps maintain a sense of closeness.

Dialogue:

- Eleanor: "I miss our time together. Let us have a home date night once a week."

- Cliff: "I would love that. How about we start this Friday?"

Support Systems: Leverage your support network, including family, friends, and professional resources. Accepting help can alleviate some of the pressures of new parenthood.

Dialogue:

- Eleanor: "My sister offered to babysit this weekend. Let us take some time for ourselves."

- Cliff: "That sounds perfect. We could really use a break."

Activities and Exercises

Activity: Couple's Reflection Time: Set aside time weekly to reflect on the week's challenges and successes. Discuss what worked well and what needs adjustment. This practice fosters open communication and continuous improvement.

Exercise: Gratitude Journaling: Maintain a shared gratitude journal where you both write down things you appreciate about each other and your parenting journey. This practice reinforces positive feelings and mutual appreciation.

Journal Entry:

- Tina "I am grateful for how you managed the midnight feeding last night. It meant a lot to me."

- Roy "I appreciate your patience and understanding when I was exhausted today. You always know how to make things better."

Reflective Practice

Self-Reflection and Growth: Engage in regular self-reflection to understand how parenthood has impacted your relationship and personal growth. Reflect on your strengths and areas for improvement.

Example Reflection Prompts:

- How has becoming a parent changed my perception of my partner?

- What qualities do I admire in my partner's parenting?

- How can I contribute more effectively to our partnership and parenting?

Conclusion

Bringing a baby home is a transformative experience that profoundly reshapes the dynamics of a relationship. By prioritizing communication, shared responsibilities, and maintaining intimacy, couples can navigate this transition with resilience and mutual support. Engaging in reflective practices and leveraging support systems further strengthens the bond between partners, creating a nurturing environment for both the baby and the relationship. Embracing this journey together not only fosters personal and relational growth but also lays a solid foundation for future children to come into the family.

Remaining a couple after the arrival of children requires intentional effort and commitment. By prioritizing your relationship, scheduling regular couple times, and communicating openly, you can maintain a strong and loving bond. Remember, a healthy relationship not only benefits you but also sets a positive example for your children. Maintaining a strong couple relationship after becoming parents is essential for a healthy, happy family. By prioritizing quality time, open communication, and mutual support, couples can navigate the challenges of parenthood while keeping their connection strong. This commitment not only benefits the partnership but also creates a nurturing and stable environment for their children to flourish.

References

- Parkes, A., Green, M., & Mitchell, K. (2019). Coparenting and parenting pathways from the couple's relationship to children's behaviour problems. Journal of Family Psychology, 33(2), 215–225. https://doi.org/10.1037/fam0000492

- Bodenmann, G. (1997). Dyadic coping - a systemic-transactional view of stress and coping among couples: Theory and empirical findings. European Review of Applied Psychology, 47(2), 137-140.

- Randall, A. K., & Bodenmann, G. (2009). The role of stress on close relationships and marital satisfaction. Clinical Psychology Review, 29(2), 105-115. https://doi.org/10.1016/j.cpr.2008.10.004

- Weir, K. (2018, September 1). What makes teams work? Monitor on Psychology, 49(8). Retrieved from https://www.apa.org/monitor/2018/09/cover-teams.

- Biehhle, S. N., & Mickelson, K. D. (2012). First-time parents' expectations about the division of childcare and play. Journal of Family Psychology, 26(1), 36-45.

- Grote, N. K., & Clark, M. S. (2001). Perceived fairness of the division of household labour and psychological distress. Journal of Marriage and Family, 63(3), 554-570.

- Lawrence, E., Rothman, A. D., Cobb, R. J., Rothman, M. T., & Bradbury, T. N. (2008). Marital satisfaction across the transition to parenthood. Journal of Family Psychology, 22(1), 41-50.

- Mindell, J. A., & Williamson, A. A. (2018). Benefits of a bedtime routine in young children: Sleep, development, and beyond. Sleep Medicine Reviews, 40, 93-108.

- Shapiro, A. F., & Gottman, J. M. (2005). Effects on the marriage of a psycho-communicative-educational intervention with couples undergoing the transition to parenthood, evaluation at 1-year post-intervention. Journal of Family Communication, 5(1), 1-24.

Chapter 2

Unified Parenting: Navigating the Challenges with Toddlers and Teens

Parenting can be a complex journey, especially during the formative years of toddlers and teens. Unified parenting emphasizes the importance of a cohesive and collaborative approach to raising children. This chapter explores strategies to maintain consistency, address disciplinary challenges, and foster a supportive environment. By aligning parenting philosophies and techniques, couples can create a stable, nurturing atmosphere that promotes the well-being of their children and strengthens the family unit.

"The strength of a family, like the strength of an army, lies in its loyalty to each other." — Mario Puzo

In the dance of parenthood, we find our stride, unified in purpose, standing side by side.

From a toddler's first steps to a teen's bold dream, Together, we navigate life's flowing stream.

Introduction

Unified parenting is a vital approach to raising children, emphasizing the importance of consistency and collaboration. This method ensures that children receive clear, unwavering guidance and support, which is especially crucial during the turbulent stages of toddlerhood and adolescence. Toddlers and teens present unique challenges and developmental needs, requiring parents to adapt and align their strategies.

In this chapter, we will delve into the principles of unified parenting, exploring how couples can maintain a cohesive front despite differing opinions or external pressures. We'll discuss practical techniques for effective communication, setting boundaries, and fostering a supportive environment that nurtures the growth and well-being of both toddlers and teens.

Parenting is a journey that requires unity, cooperation, and mutual support. By working together as a team, couples can navigate the challenges of parenting while maintaining a strong and loving relationship. Unified parenting not only benefits the children but also strengthens the bond between partners.

Understanding Unified Parenting

When John and Corinne welcomed their first child, they quickly realized the importance of presenting a unified front in their parenting approach. Unified parenting offers a foundation of stability and predictability, which is essential for children's emotional and psychological development. By working together cohesively, they provided consistent expectations and reinforced trust within their family unit. This unified approach helped their children understand boundaries and consequences, fostering a sense of security.

Impact on Family Dynamics

A consistent parenting approach significantly strengthens their overall family dynamic, reducing conflicts and misunderstandings. When John and Corinne aligned their strategies, it created a harmonious environment where their children knew what to expect and felt supported. This reduced stress for both parents and children, enhancing the overall family experience.

However, when parents are not aligned, children may feel confused about how to express their emotions, receiving mixed signals that lead to uncertainty about whether it's safe to talk about their feelings. This can create periods of tension and unresolved conflicts. With conscious effort and understanding, John and Corinne worked together to create a balanced approach that incorporated both open communication and respect for each other's comfort levels.

Developing a Parenting Philosophy

Crafting a shared parenting philosophy was crucial for John and Corrine. They spent time discussing their values, goals, and disciplinary methods to align their approaches and create a unified strategy that supported their children's growth and development.

Practical Strategies for Unified Parenting

Open Communication

John and Corrine maintained regular, open dialogues about their parenting decisions. They scheduled weekly check-ins to discuss any issues or adjustments needed, ensuring they were always on the same page and could address concerns proactively.

Dialogue

Daniel: "I've noticed that our toddler is struggling with bedtime routines. How do you feel about adjusting our approach?"

Tess: "Yes, it would be good to understand what the issues are. Maybe getting help from Ngala or other sleep specialists might help. Don't you think we have tried many approaches, like turning on the white noise, rocking the cradle, stopping stimulation, wrapping the baby, and keeping the room warm?"

Daniel: "I agree. Let's try a consistent bedtime routine and perhaps get some professional help as well."

Unified Decisions

Daniel and Tess presented decisions as a team to their children, reinforcing the idea that both parents were equally authoritative and supportive. They avoided undermining each other's authority in front of their kids.

Dialogue

Sherman: "We've decided that screen time will be limited to one hour a day. We need to stick with this decision, even if it means we have to monitor the routine for a while. We can't give our child mixed messages."

Cristina: "Yes, I know I sometimes want to give in to his sweet requests, but we both need to be on the same page. We can use that time for educational, music, and sports activities. Your parents will be happy with that too."

Consistency in Discipline

Sherman and Cristina established clear and consistent disciplinary measures, agreeing on rules and consequences, and ensuring they were enforced uniformly.

Dialogue

Farah: "We need to be consistent with our teenager's curfew. How about we set a firm 10 PM limit on school nights?"

Chris: "That sounds fair. We should also discuss the consequences if the curfew is broken. We can start them on some spiritual and extra religious classes that Mom and Dad mentioned. Our parents said it would imbibe the right values and morals. In today's world, every aspect that points to our children in the right direction and keeps them there would help."

Farah: "I do understand where you're coming from. While we are good at setting rules, we also need to give them a value-based education from home".

Supportive Environment

Chris and Farah created a home environment that encouraged open communication and mutual respect. They modelled positive behaviours and demonstrated how to manage conflicts constructively.

Dialogue

Sheldon: "I appreciate how we calmly discussed the issues with our teens today. I know I usually get reactive, and you really helped support me."

Needlyn: "It really helps when we show them how to manage disagreements respectfully."

Scenario

Your toddler throws a tantrum in a public place.

Sheldon: "Let's calmly address their needs and guide them to a quieter spot."

Needlyn: "I agree. They might act up in front of others, but we will stay firm and in control, being assertive yet gentle. This will help them understand boundaries."

Scenario

Fumiko and Hoshi are a married couple with two children. Hoshi grew up in a family where open communication and emotional expression were encouraged. His parents always discussed their feelings and resolved conflicts through calm conversations. On the other hand, Fumiko was raised in a family where emotions were rarely discussed, especially around sensitive topics, and conflicts were often avoided or resolved through passive-aggressive behaviour.

Hoshi encourages his children to talk about their feelings and believes in resolving conflicts through discussion. Fumiko, however, struggles with encouraging emotional expression in her children and finds it difficult to discuss emotions openly.

Dialogue

Hoshi: "Fumiko, I've noticed that we have different ways of handling discipline. I think it's important for us to be consistent with the kids."

Fumiko: "I agree, Hoshi. Let us talk about our approaches and find a way to combine them. We need to be on the same page."

Hoshi: "Absolutely. I believe in setting clear boundaries and using positive reinforcement. What about you?"

Fumiko: "I think structure is important, but I also want to make sure we're being fair and understanding. We need to create harmony, agree on certain aspects, and know that we want the best for our kids. Let's create a plan that incorporates both our views and perhaps trial different strategies to see which one works."

Hoshi: "Sounds good. We'll need to communicate regularly to make sure we're staying consistent."

Through open dialogue, unified decision-making, and consistent discipline, John and Emily, along with Fumiko and Hoshi, exemplify how unified parenting can create a stable, harmonious, and supportive family environment. Their commitment to understanding and aligning their parenting approaches ensures their children grow up feeling secure, supported, and loved.

Example Discussion Points:

- What values are most important to us as a family?

- How do we want to oversee discipline and conflict resolution?

- What are our goals for our children's development?

Exercise: Role-Playing Scenarios: Practice role-playing various scenarios to develop a consistent response strategy. This helps both parents feel prepared and confident in handling real-life situations.

Reflective Practice

Self-Reflection and Growth: Engage in regular self-reflection to understand how your unified parenting approach impacts your children and your relationship. Reflect on your strengths and areas for improvement.

Reflection Prompts:

- How has our unified approach benefited our family dynamic?

- What challenges have we faced in maintaining consistency?

- What adjustments can we make to improve our parenting strategy?

Activities and Exercises

Activity: Parenting Philosophy Workshop: Set aside time to discuss and document your parenting philosophy. Cover topics such as discipline, education, social values, and emotional support. This exercise helps solidify a unified approach.

Conclusion

Unified parenting is essential for creating a stable and nurturing environment for children, especially during the formative years of toddlers and teens. By prioritizing consistency, open communication, and a collaborative approach, parents can effectively navigate the challenges of these developmental stages. This unified strategy not only supports the growth and well-being of children but also strengthens parental relationships, fostering a cohesive and harmonious family dynamic.

References

1. Baumrind, D. (1991). The influence of parenting style on adolescent competence and substance use. Journal of Early Adolescence, 11(1), 56-95.

2. Darling, N., & Steinberg, L. (1993). Parenting style as context: An integrative model. Psychological Bulletin, 113(3), 487-496.

3. Maccoby, E. E., & Martin, J. A. (1983). Socialization in the context of the family: Parent-child interaction. In P. H. Mussen (Ed.), Handbook of child psychology (Vol. 4, pp. 1-101). New York: Wiley.

4. Patterson, G. R. (1982). Coercive family process. Eugene, OR: Castalia Publishing Company.

5. Simons, R. L., Whitbeck, L. B., Conger, R. D., & Conger, K. J. (1991). Parenting factors, social skills, and value commitments as precursors to school failure, involvement with deviant peers, and delinquent behaviour. Journal of Youth and Adolescence, 20(6), 645-664.

Chapter 3

Nurturing Souls: The Role of Faith and Spirituality in Parenting

Faith and spirituality can play a significant role in shaping family values, guiding principles, and parenting practices. This chapter explores how integrating faith and spirituality into parenting can provide a moral framework, offer emotional support, and strengthen family bonds. Discover ways to cultivate a spiritual environment that nurtures the growth and development of children while respecting individual beliefs and fostering open-mindedness.

"Family is the first school for young children, and parents are powerful models." — *Alice Sterling Honig.*

In faith, we find a guiding light,

A beacon through the darkest night.

With love and grace, our hearts we mould,

A family's spirit, strong and bold.

Introduction

Faith and spirituality offer a profound foundation for family life, providing moral guidance, emotional support, and a sense of purpose. For many families, these elements are integral to their identity and daily practices. Integrating faith into parenting can help instill values, foster resilience, and build a keen sense of community.

This chapter delves into several ways faith and spirituality can influence parenting, from establishing rituals and traditions to navigating challenges with grace and compassion. We will explore practical strategies for integrating these elements into family life while also respecting the diverse beliefs and spiritual practices of all family members. Faith is a deeply personal and often sensitive topic, yet it plays a crucial role in many relationships. Open and respectful conversations about faith can strengthen the bond between partners, foster mutual understanding, and provide a solid foundation for navigating life's challenges together. This chapter explores how couples can discuss their faith, respect each other's beliefs, and integrate their spiritual practices into their relationship.

Understanding the Role of Faith and Spirituality in Parenting

Faith and spirituality play a pivotal role in parenting, offering a moral and ethical framework that guides decisions and behaviours. For many families, faith helps impart values such as honesty, kindness, compassion, and integrity to their children. Let us take a closer look at how these elements can enrich family life through the story of several families.

Moral and Ethical Foundation

Meet the Patel family. When it comes to instructing their children about right and wrong, they rely heavily on the teachings from their faith. Values like honesty, kindness, and integrity are discussed during their nightly family prayers. This consistent reinforcement helps their children develop a strong moral compass.

Emotional and Psychological Support

Faith can also provide emotional and psychological support. During challenging times, the Fernandez family turns to their spirituality for comfort and strength. When facing tough decisions or personal hardships, they gather for a prayer or meditation session, which offers them hope, purpose, and resilience. This practice helps them navigate life's challenges with a positive outlook.

Community and Belonging

Faith-based communities offer a supportive network that enhances a family's sense of belonging and connection. The Johnsons actively participate in their local church, where they find mentorship, social support, and a sense of community. These connections enrich their family life, providing both parents and children with a broader support system.

Spiritual Practices and Rituals

Incorporating spiritual practices and rituals into daily life creates a sense of structure and continuity. The Watanabe family, for example, starts their day with a gratitude prayer. Each member shares one thing they are thankful for, setting a positive tone for the day. They also attend services together and celebrate religious holidays, which strengthen their family bonds and create lasting memories.

The Importance of Discussing Faith

Discussing faith within the family helps identify and reinforce shared values. This unity fosters a cohesive family dynamic and provides a strong moral compass for decision-making. In the case of the Ahmed family, regular discussions about their faith help them align core values and principles, guiding their actions and decisions.

Mutual Respect

Respecting each other's beliefs is crucial, especially in families with diverse spiritual backgrounds. Open discussions about faith promote understanding and empathy, allowing family members to honour and appreciate their differences. In the Parker family, where one parent is Christian and the other is Jewish, they encourage open dialogue and respect each other's practices, creating a harmonious environment.

Emotional Support

Faith can be a cornerstone of emotional support, offering comfort and solace in times of stress. Families that share and discuss their spiritual beliefs can draw strength from their faith during challenging periods. The Khans, for example, find solace in their shared spiritual practices, which help them cope with stress and support each other.

Spiritual Growth

Engaging in spiritual practices together fosters spiritual growth. This shared journey enhances the family bond and helps children develop a deeper understanding of their faith. The Larsons, for instance, have weekly family devotionals that provide an opportunity for reflection and spiritual discussion, deepening their connection.

The Benefits of Two Faiths

Having two faiths within a family can be enriching, offering diverse perspectives and a broader understanding of spirituality. This diversity encourages open-mindedness and mutual respect, providing children with a well-rounded spiritual education. The Bennetts, who practice both Christianity and Buddhism, incorporate traditions from both faiths, enriching their children's spiritual upbringing.

Practical Strategies for Integrating Faith into Daily Life

Integrating Faith into Daily Life

Families can find ways to incorporate spiritual practices into everyday routines. This could include morning prayers, bedtime stories with moral lessons, or expressing gratitude before meals.

Dialogue with Glenn and Juliet

Glenn: "Let's start each day with a gratitude prayer. It'll set a positive tone for the day."

Juliet: "I love that idea. We can each share one thing we're grateful for."

Glenn: "It's important to inculcate good practices for our children, and they always need to know there is something bigger than us earthlings."

Respecting Individual Beliefs

Encouraging open discussions about faith and spirituality is essential. Respect each family member's beliefs and experiences, creating an environment where everyone feels valued and heard.

Example Dialogue with Farah and Chris

Farah: "I know we all have different ways of connecting with our faith. Let's respect each other's practices and learn from them."

Zubin: "Agreed. We can each share our unique traditions and find common ground."

Farah: "Instead of choosing between our faiths, I think it is wise for the children to learn both and then choose what they feel more comfortable with. They may even want to adopt both of our faiths."

Zubin: "I think that is a great idea."

Navigating Different Beliefs

In families where one partner has faith and the other does not, it's essential to find common ground and respect each other's perspectives.

Example Dialogue with Pearl and Johan

Pearl: "I find comfort in my faith and would like to share some practices with our children."

Johan: "I respect that. Let's make sure they also have the freedom to explore and choose their own beliefs."

Creating Spiritual Traditions

Establish family traditions that reflect your spiritual beliefs. These could include weekly family devotionals, attending religious services together, or participating in community service projects. Youssef and Bina, who come from different religious backgrounds, decided to have regular discussions about their beliefs and how they wanted to incorporate their faiths into their family life. This helped them respect each other's traditions and find common ground.

Dialogue

Youssef: "Linda, I know we come from different religious backgrounds, but I think it's important for us to talk about our faith and how we want to incorporate it into our lives."

Linda: "I agree, Youssef. I respect your beliefs, and I want us to find a way to honour both of our traditions. Let's start by sharing what our faith means to us and how we practice it."

Youssef: "That sounds good. I think we can also explore ways to celebrate our faiths together, like attending each other's services or creating new traditions."

Linda: "Absolutely. I believe this will help us understand each other better and strengthen our relationship."

Dialogue

Paul: "How about we volunteer at the local shelter as a family once a month?"

Daisy: "Great idea. I have always wanted to add something more meaningful to our lives as a thanksgiving for all we have received from God. It'll be a meaningful way to live out our values and help others."

Activities and Exercises

Activity: Family Faith Reflection

Set aside time for a family discussion about what faith and spirituality mean to each member. Encourage everyone to share their thoughts and experiences.

Example Reflection Questions

- What role does faith play in our family?
- How do our spiritual beliefs shape our values and actions?
- What are some spiritual practices we can incorporate into our

daily lives?

- How did discussing your faith impact your relationship?
- What did you learn about your partner's beliefs and values?
- How can you continue to respect and support each other's spiritual journeys?

Exercise: Gratitude Journal

Maintain a family gratitude journal where everyone writes down things for which they are thankful. Reflect on these entries together regularly to foster a sense of appreciation and positivity.

Understanding the Role of Faith and Spirituality in Parenting

Moral and Ethical Foundation: Faith often provides a moral and ethical framework that guides parenting decisions and behaviours. It helps parents impart values such as honesty, kindness, compassion, and integrity to their children.

Emotional and Psychological Support: Spirituality can be a source of comfort and strength during challenging times. It offers a sense of hope, purpose, and resilience, helping families navigate challenges with a positive outlook.

Community and Belonging:

Faith-based communities provide a supportive network that can enhance a family's sense of belonging and connection. These communities often offer resources, mentorship, and social support that enrich family life.

Spiritual Practices and Rituals:

Incorporating spiritual practices and rituals into daily life can create a sense of structure and continuity. Activities such as prayer, meditation, attending services, and celebrating religious holidays can strengthen family bonds and create lasting memories.

Practical Strategies:

Integrating Faith into Daily Life: Find ways to incorporate spiritual practices into everyday routines. This could include morning prayers, bedtime stories with moral lessons, or expressing gratitude before meals.

Conclusion

Faith and spirituality offer a rich tapestry of guidance, support, and community that can profoundly impact parenting. By integrating these elements into family life, parents can instill values, foster resilience, and create a nurturing environment for their children. Respecting individual beliefs and fostering open dialogue ensures that spirituality becomes a source of unity and strength for the entire family.

Conversations about faith are essential for building a strong and respectful relationship. By discussing your beliefs, identifying shared values, and integrating spiritual practices into your life, you can enhance your emotional and spiritual connection. Remember, mutual respect and open communication are key to navigating differences and fostering a harmonious relationship.

References

- Boyatzis, C. J. (2003). Religious and spiritual development in childhood. In Handbook of the Psychology of Religion and Spirituality (pp. 123-143). New York, NY: Guilford Press.

- Dollahite, D. C., & Marks, L. D. (2009). A conceptual model of family and religious processes in highly religious families. Review of Religious Research, 50(4), 373-391.

- Mahoney, A., Pargament, K. I., Tarakeshwar, N., & Swank, A. B. (2001). Religion in the home in the 1980s and 1990s: A meta-analytic review and conceptual analysis of links between religion, marriage, and parenting. Journal of Family Psychology, 15(4), 559-596.

- Roehlkepartain, E. C., King, P. E., Wagener, L., & Benson, P. L. (Eds.). (2006). The Handbook of spiritual development in childhood and adolescence. Thousand Oaks, CA: Sage Publications.

- Walsh, F. (2009). Spiritual resources in family therapy. New York, NY: Guilford Press.

- Ellison, C. G., & Levin, J. S. (1998). The religion-health connection: Evidence, theory, and future directions. Health Education & Behaviour, 25(6), 700-720. https://doi.org/10.1177/109019819802500603

- Koenig, H. G. (2012). Religion, spirituality, and health: The research and clinical implications. ISRN Psychiatry, 2012, 278730. https://doi.org/10.5402/2012/278730

- Pargament, K. I. (1997). The psychology of religion and coping: Theory, research, practice. Guilford Press.

Module 4
The Gentle Approach: Tackling Tough Topics with Grace

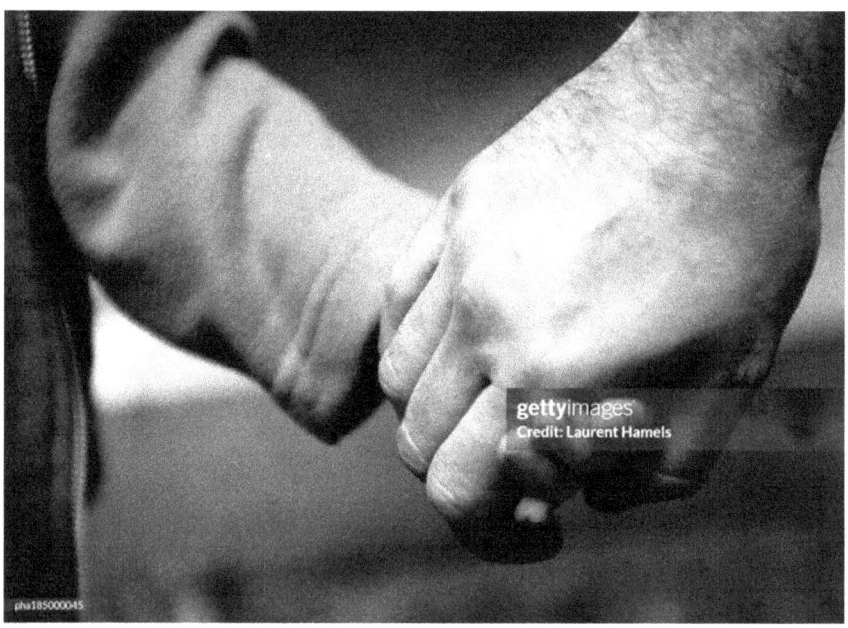

Chapter 1

Heartstrings and Healing: Loving Someone with Addictions

Loving Someone with Addictions delves into the profound emotional journey of loving a partner who struggles with addiction. It explores the delicate balance between compassion and self-preservation, offering insights into the complexities of such relationships. The book provides practical advice on setting boundaries, seeking support, and fostering resilience while maintaining hope and love.

Addiction is a family disease. One person may use, but the whole family suffers."

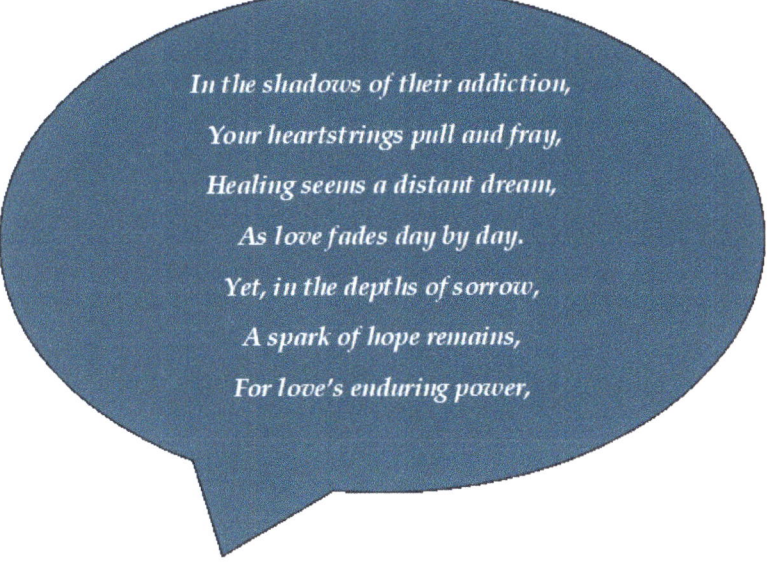

In the shadows of their addiction,

Your heartstrings pull and fray,

Healing seems a distant dream,

As love fades day by day.

Yet, in the depths of sorrow,

A spark of hope remains,

For love's enduring power,

Introduction

Falling in love with someone who struggles with alcohol or drug addiction can be a complex and challenging journey. Addiction not only affects the individual but also has profound impacts on their relationships. Understanding the dynamics of addiction and its effects on a partnership is crucial for navigating these challenges and fostering a supportive and healthy relationship.

Loving someone who needs to heal from addiction is an immense challenge that demands a deep well of compassion, patience, and resilience. Take the story of Mark and Lisa. Mark loves Lisa deeply, but her struggle with addiction has brought trust issues, financial instability, and emotional turmoil into their lives. Mark knows that navigating this journey requires empathy and a willingness to seek help for both Lisa and him.

Understanding Addiction

Understanding that addiction is a chronic disease, not a moral failing, is crucial. It's characterized by an inability to stop using a substance despite harmful consequences. Mark learns about the science of addiction, realizing it affects the brain's reward, motivation, and memory functions. This knowledge helps him approach Lisa with empathy, rather than judgment.

Communication and Boundaries

Open and honest communication becomes their lifeline. One evening, Mark sits down with Lisa and gently says, "Lisa, I'm really concerned about your health and our future. I think we need to talk about how we can manage this together." Setting clear boundaries is equally important. Mark explains, "I love you, but I can't support your substance use. We need to find healthier ways to cope."

Seeking Support

Encouraging professional help is a crucial step. Mark suggests, "How about we look into therapy or a support group? There are great programs that could help us." He also realizes he needs support, attending a group for families of addicts and seeking counselling for himself. This network provides him with the strength to continue supporting Lisa while taking care of his own well-being.

Self-Care

Taking care of himself is essential for Mark. He finds solace in his hobbies, like running and painting, making sure to carve out time for these activities. He reminds himself, "I can't pour from an empty cup. To help Lisa, I need to be strong and healthy too."

Considering Before Marriage or Long-Term Commitment

Before deciding on marriage or a long-term commitment, Mark and Lisa have open discussions about the challenges they face. Mark says, "We need to think about how addiction might impact our future together, from our finances to our emotional health." They consider premarital counselling to address these issues and set realistic expectations.

Starting a Family

As they contemplate starting a family, Mark and Lisa evaluate their readiness to provide a stable and healthy environment for children. Mark expresses his concerns, "Addiction can really affect parenting and family dynamics. We both need to be committed to seeking help and maintaining sobriety for the sake of our future children."

Through empathy, open communication, and a commitment to seeking help, Mark and Lisa navigate the complexities of loving someone who needs to heal from addiction. Their journey is challenging, but with mutual support and understanding, they work towards a healthier and more stable future together.

Dialogue:

Sheila: "Jason, I've noticed that your drinking has worsened, and I'm really worried about you."

Jason: "I know, Sheila, I've been struggling, but I don't know how to stop."

Sheila: "I love you, and I want to support you. Have you thought about seeking help? Some programs and therapists specialize in addiction."

Jason: "I am scared, but I think I need to do something. I do not want to lose you."

Sheila: "We can do this together. I'll be here for you every step of the way, but we need to set some boundaries to protect our relationship and my well-being, too."

Jason: "I understand. I will investigate getting help. Thank you for standing by me."

Sheila: "Also, before we think about marriage or starting a family, we need to make sure we're both in a good place. I want us to have a strong foundation."

Jason: "You're right. I want that, too. Let's take it one step at a time."

Bringing a child into a world of uncertainty and undue risk is not advisable. Couples need to address all the problems or illnesses to ensure a risk-free pregnancy and save future children from the consequences of parents with addictions. It is a grave and complex problem that spirals out of control and adds layers of other complications that are even more problematic to solve.

Dialogue:

Sharon and Reggie have been married for over 21 years, and Reggie has been a fantastic father to his children and a good husband and breadwinner. However, staying away from the family for prolonged periods caused him to resort to alcoholism to reduce his work stress. His boss had been very patient and understanding for a long time; however, he had warned him of dire consequences if he did not take active and urgent measures to reduce his drinking. He tried giving up; however, he kept refusing to go to rehab until his wife decided to take matters into her own hands.

Sharon: Reggie, we need to talk. I love you, but things cannot go on like this.

Reggie: I know, Sharon. I have been trying to get a handle on things, but it is hard.

Sharon: I understand it is difficult, but your addiction is tearing our family apart. You have lost your job, and now the house is re-mortgaged. I'm scared for our future.

Reggie: I never wanted to hurt you or the kids. I feel like I am drowning, and I do not know how to stop.

Sharon: We were childhood sweethearts, Reggie. I have always believed in us, but I cannot do this alone. We need help. You need help.

Reggie: I am afraid, Sharon. What if I cannot change?

Sharon: We will face it together, but you must take the first step. There are programs and support groups. We can find a way out of this darkness.

Reggie: I do not want to lose you or the kids. I will do whatever it takes. I promise.

Sharon: Promises are a start, but actions speak louder. Let us plan. Tomorrow, we will investigate treatment options. We cannot afford to wait any longer.

Reggie: Thank you for not giving up on me. I will do better for you and our family.

Sharon: We will get through this, Reggie. One step at a time. I love you, and I believe in us. Let us start by finding a rehab program that can help you get back on track.

Reggie: I will do it, Sharon. I will join a rehab program. I want to be the husband and father you deserve.

Sharon: And while you are in rehab, I will join Al-Anon meetings. They can help me understand how to support you better and cope with my own feelings. We can both get the support we need.

Reggie: That sounds like a promising idea. Knowing you are getting support, too, makes me feel less alone in this.

Sharon: We are doing this together, Reggie. We will both get the help we need, and we will come out stronger on the other side.

Unfortunately, months later, this case turned out to be a disaster. Reggie died of liver failure, and Sharon was left to take care of debts and the two children all by herself.

Self-Reflections

1. **Reflect on Your Boundaries:** Consider what boundaries you need to set to protect your well-being. Write them down and discuss them with your partner.

2. **Identify Support Systems:** List the people and resources you can turn to for support. This might include friends, family, support groups, or professional counsellors.

3. **Personal Well-being:** Reflect on activities that help you relax and recharge. Plan to incorporate these into your routine regularly.

4. **Future Planning:** Consider your long-term goals and how addiction might impact them. Discuss these with your partner to ensure you are both on the same page.

Conclusion

Navigating a relationship with someone who has an addiction is undoubtedly challenging, but it is not insurmountable. Open communication, empathy, and professional support are key to managing these difficulties. By addressing addiction openly and honestly, setting clear boundaries, and seeking help, couples can build a foundation of trust and resilience. It is crucial to consider these factors before making long-term commitments or starting a family to ensure a stable and healthy future together. Remember, love and support can make a significant difference, but self-care and professional guidance are equally important in this journey.

References

1. Psychology Today discusses the impact of addiction on relationships and the importance of recovery support.

2. Psych Central highlights the challenges of repairing relationships affected by substance use disorder and the importance of rebuilding trust.

3. American Addiction Centres emphasizes the role of supportive relationships in recovery and maintaining sobriety.

4. BMC Psychiatry provides a systematic review of the relationship between interpersonal trauma and addictive behaviours.

5. International Journal of Mental Health and Addiction explores the lived experience of co-dependency, which is often present in relationships affected by addiction.

Chapter 2

Navigating Life's Final Chapters: Aging, Death, Will, and Related Matters

Discussing aging, death, and related legal matters can be daunting, yet it is crucial for ensuring peace of mind and fulfilling final wishes. This chapter explores how couples can approach these difficult conversations with empathy, clarity, and foresight. Learn strategies for discussing wills, healthcare decisions, and end-of-life preferences in a way that honours each person's values and alleviates uncertainties for loved ones.

"In the end, it's not the years in your life that count; it's the life in your years." — *Abraham Lincoln.*

In the whispers of time, we weave our tale,

Through aging's path and final sail.

With love and grace, we plan ahead,

Introduction:

Conversations about aging, death, and related legal matters are among the most challenging but necessary discussions couples can have. Addressing these topics openly and thoughtfully ensures that final wishes are respected and loved ones cared for. This chapter provides guidance on navigating these sensitive issues with compassion and clarity, helping couples make informed decisions that bring peace of mind.

We will cover strategies for discussing aging, healthcare preferences, wills, and end-of-life plans, emphasizing the importance of mutual respect and understanding. By approaching these topics proactively, couples can strengthen their bond and create a   legacy of love and preparedness.

The Importance of Discussing Aging, Death, and Related Matters

When Kevin and Kerry sat down for their regular Sunday chat, they knew it was time to discuss some difficult but essential topics. Preparing for aging and end-of-life issues is an emotional journey, but it helps reduce anxiety and emotional distress. These discussions allow individuals like Kevin and Kerry to express their wishes and ensure their needs are met, providing a sense of control and comfort. It helps alleviate fears, clarify wishes, and ensures their loved ones are not left with complex decisions during emotional times.

Emotional Preparation

During their talk, Kerry expressed her concerns about aging and the end-of-life care she wanted. "Kevin, I want to make sure that my wishes are clear, so our kids don't have to make tough decisions when the time comes," she said. This open conversation helped them both feel more prepared and less anxious about the future.

Legal and Financial Clarity

Kevin and Kerry knew that discussing wills, healthcare directives, and financial plans was crucial to prevent confusion and conflicts among family members. They sat down with a lawyer to ensure their wishes were legally documented. "Having everything in writing will make things easier for everyone," Kevin noted. This clarity ensured that decisions would be made in accordance with their desires.

Strengthening Relationships

Open conversations about aging and end-of-life matters deepened trust and understanding between Kevin and Kerry. These discussions fostered a sense of mutual support and shared responsibility, reinforcing the strength of their relationship. "Talking about these things brings us closer," Kerry said, feeling the bond with Kevin grow stronger.

Wills and Estate Planning

Creating a will and planning their estate were crucial steps for Max and Annie. They wanted to ensure that their assets would be distributed according to their wishes. "This will prevent any disputes among our children," Max explained. They also considered setting up trusts, designating beneficiaries, and evaluating tax implications to manage their estate effectively.

Health Care Directives

Health care directives, such as living wills and durable powers of attorney for health care, allowed Max and Annie to specify their medical treatment preferences if they could not make decisions for themselves. Annie shared,

"It's a relief to know that my wishes will be followed, and it will spare you from making tough choices on my behalf."

Terminal Illness

Facing a terminal illness is one of the most challenging situations for families. Max and Annie understood the importance of having compassionate and clear conversations about end-of-life care preferences, pain management, and emotional support. They discussed their wishes for quality of life, palliative care options, and the emotional needs of both the patient and their loved ones. "Having these conversations early will help us be better prepared," Max remarked, knowing it would provide comfort and clarity during grim times.

The Consequences of Non-Disclosure

Max and Annie also recognized the severe consequences of not discussing significant concerns like mental health issues. They knew that undisclosed issues could lead to misunderstandings, mistrust, and a lack of support. Annie said, "Keeping things hidden only makes it worse. We need to be open to get the help we need." This openness prevented conditions from worsening and ensured they had the necessary support.

Through these discussions, Max and Annie found themselves better prepared for the future. They understood the importance of addressing aging, death, and related matters early on. This initiative-taking approach not only provided them with peace of mind but also strengthened their relationship, ensuring they were ready to support each other through any challenges life might bring.

Actual Conversations

Conversation 1: Discussing Aging and Health Care Preferences

Betty: "Dad, I've been thinking a lot about the future, and I want to ensure we know your wishes for health care."

Dad: "I appreciate that, Betty. I have been meaning to talk to you about it, too. I want to stay at home as long as possible, but if I need more care, I'd prefer a good nursing home."

Betty: "That makes sense. Have you thought about a living will or a health care proxy?"

Dad: "Yes, I have. I would like you to be my healthcare proxy. I trust you to make the right decisions if I can't."

Betty: "Thank you, Dad. I will make sure your wishes are respected."

Conversation 2: Planning a Will

Richard: "Peta, we need to talk about our will and estate planning. It's important to make sure everything is in order."

Peta "I agree, Richard. We should decide how we want to distribute our assets and who will be the guardian for the kids if something happens to us."

Richard "Exactly. Let us set up a meeting with a lawyer to get everything documented properly."

Peta: "Good idea. It will give us peace of mind knowing everything is taken care of."

Conversation 3: Addressing End-of-Life Wishes

Vincent: "Alice, I know this is a tough topic, but we need to talk about our end-of-life wishes."

Alice: "I know, Vincent, it is important. I want to make sure we both know what the other wants."

Vincent: "Exactly. I will prefer to be at home with hospice care if it comes to that. What about you?"

Alice: "I feel the same way. And I think we should also discuss our funeral preferences and make sure our wills are up to date."

Vincent: "Agreed. Let us make an appointment to get everything in order."

Activity: Reflect and Act

1. **Reflection:** Take some time to consider your wishes regarding aging, health care, and end-of-life preferences. Write down your thoughts and discuss them with your partner or family.

2. **Action:** Create or update your will and health care directives. Schedule a meeting with a lawyer to ensure all legal documents are in place and reflect your current wishes.

Self-Reflections

1. **Personal Wishes:** Reflect on your wishes for aging, health care, and end-of-life care. How do you want to be cared for, and what are your priorities?

2. **Support Systems:** Identify the people and resources you can turn to for support. This might include family, friends, health care providers, or legal professionals.

3. **Future Planning:** Think about your long-term goals and how you can ensure they are met. Discuss these plans with your loved ones to ensure everyone is on the same page.

Reflective Practice

Self-Reflection and Growth: Regularly self-reflect on aging, death, and your wishes. Reflect on how these conversations impact your relationship and personal growth.

Example Reflection Prompts:

How do I feel about discussing aging and end-of-life matters?

What are my main concerns and wishes for the future?

How can I support my partner in these discussions?

Conclusion

Conversations about aging, death, and wills are essential for ensuring that our wishes are respected, and our loved ones are prepared. By addressing these topics openly and honestly, we can alleviate fears, clarify our wishes, and provide peace of mind for ourselves and our families. Planning for the future is an act of love and responsibility that can strengthen relationships and ensure a smoother transition during challenging times. Proactive planning provides peace of mind and strengthens the bond between partners, leaving a legacy of love and preparedness.

References

- Psychology Today discusses the importance of relationships in aging and the role of social support systems1.

- Mayo Clinic highlights the benefits of strong social connections for healthy aging2.

- BMC Nursing explores older persons' thoughts about death and dying and their experiences of care in end-of-life3.

- Oxford Academic provides insights into advanced care planning and its importance in end-of-life care4.

- Cambridge University Press reviews the concept of ethical wills and their role in leaving a lasting legacy5.

- Carr, D., & Khodyakov, D. (2007). End-of-life health care planning among young-old adults: An assessment of psychosocial influences. Journal of Gerontology: Social Sciences, 62B (2), S135-S141.

- Doka, K. J. (2002). Living with grief: Loss in later life. Washington, DC: Hospice Foundation of America.

- Lynn, J., & Harrold, J. (1999). Handbook for Mortals: Guidance for People Facing Serious Illness. New York: Oxford University Press.

- Palliative Care: The Principles of Symptom Management and End-of-Life Care. (2009). National Hospice and Palliative Care Organization.

- Steinhauser, K. E., Christakis, N. A., Clipp, E. C., McNeilly, M., McIntyre, L., & Tulsky, J. A. (2000). Factors considered important at the end of life by patients, family, physicians, and other care providers. JAMA, 284(19), 2476-2482.

Chapter 3

Navigating Mental Health Conversations: Ensuring Support and Understanding

Discussing mental health can be a sensitive but vital conversation in any relationship. This chapter explores how couples can approach these discussions with compassion, understanding, and effective communication. Learn strategies for recognizing signs of mental health struggles, offering support, and seeking professional help. By fostering a safe and open environment, couples can ensure that mental health is prioritized and addressed with the care they deserve.

"Mental health is not a destination, but a process. It's about how you drive, not where you're going." — Noam Spancer, Ph.D.

In the storm's embrace, you find your strength,

For within you lies a light of endless length.

Though shadows may fall and clouds may loom,

Remember, you are the sun that breaks the gloom!

Introduction

Mental health is critical to overall well-being, and its impact on relationships cannot be overstated. When one or both partners struggle with mental health issues, it can create significant challenges. However, couples can navigate these difficulties together with understanding, open communication, and the right support. This chapter explores the importance of addressing mental health in relationships, providing practical advice, real-

life conversations, and reflections to help couples manage these situ
Understanding Mental Health in Relationships

Understanding Mental Health in Relationships

For Susan and Jack, recognizing and addressing mental health issues has been a crucial part of maintaining their relationship. Mental health conditions such as depression, anxiety, and bipolar disorder can profoundly affect relationships, leading to misunderstandings, emotional distance, and conflicts. Susan noticed that Jack had been more withdrawn lately, not sleeping well, and losing interest in activities he used to enjoy. Recognizing these signs and symptoms early is the first step in addressing them, and it's essential to approach these conversations with empathy and without judgment.

Recognizing the Signs

Susan's awareness of Jack's changes in mood, behaviour, sleep patterns, and appetite was key. Being attuned to these signs allowed them to address the issues before they escalated. She gently brought it up one evening, "Jack, I've noticed you haven't been yourself lately. How are you feeling?"

Reducing Stigma

Open conversations about mental health help reduce the stigma associated with mental illness. Susan and Jack made it a point to normalize these discussions, fostering an environment where they felt safe to express their struggles without fear of judgment. "We're in this together, and there's no shame in talking about what we're going through," Susan reassured him.

Communication and Support

Open and honest communication became their lifeline. Jack shared his feelings, and Susan listened actively, validating his experiences. "I appreciate you telling me this. It must be really hard for you," she said. Supporting a partner with mental health issues involves patience, understanding, and sometimes encouraging them to seek professional help. Susan gently suggested, "Maybe talking to a therapist could help you navigate this."

Setting Boundaries

Establishing healthy boundaries was vital to protect both their well-being. They set limits on certain behaviours, ensured time for self-care, and sought external support when needed. "We need to make sure we're both taking care of ourselves too," Susan emphasized, scheduling regular times for activities they enjoyed separately.

Seeking Professional Help

Encouraging professional help was a crucial step. Jack agreed to see a therapist, and they also attended couple's therapy to address the impact of his mental health on their relationship. Professional guidance provided strategies and tools to manage his mental health effectively. "It's okay to ask for help, and it's helping us both," Jack admitted.

Considering Before Marriage or Long-Term Commitment

Before deciding on a long-term commitment or marriage, Susan and Jack had open discussions about their mental health. They wanted to set realistic expectations and prepare for potential difficulties. Premarital counselling proved invaluable in these discussions. "We need to be honest about our challenges and how we'll support each other," Jack said.

Starting a Family

When considering starting a family, they evaluated their readiness to provide a stable and healthy environment for children. Susan and Jack knew that mental health issues could impact parenting abilities and family dynamics. They are committed to maintaining their mental health and seeking help when needed to create a nurturing environment for future children. "Our kids deserve the best version of us," Susan expressed.

Consequences of non-disclosure

They also understood the severe consequences of not disclosing mental health issues. Undisclosed mental illness could lead to misunderstandings, mistrust, and a lack of support. This secrecy could exacerbate the condition, leading to more significant problems. "Keeping things hidden only makes it worse. We need to be open to get the help we need," Susan emphasized.

Through empathy, open communication, and a commitment to seeking help, Susan and Jack navigated the complexities of mental health in their relationship. Their journey was challenging, but with mutual support and understanding, they worked towards a healthier and more stable future together effectively.

Actual Conversations

Conversation 1: Addressing Mental Health Concerns

Jacque: "Damien, I have noticed you have been feeling down a lot lately. I am really worried about you."

Damien: "I know, Jacque. I have been struggling with anxiety, but I do not know how to talk about it."

Jacque: "It is okay to feel that way. I am here for you. Have you thought about seeing a therapist? It might help to talk to someone professional."

Damien: "I'm scared, but I think I need to do something. I don't want this to affect our relationship."

Jacque: "We can do this together. I will support you every step of the way. Let's find a therapist who can help."

Conversation 2: Setting Boundaries

Felix: "I've been feeling overwhelmed with everything lately, and I think we need to set some boundaries to protect our mental health."

Rufina: "I agree, Felix. What kind of boundaries are you thinking about?"

Felix: "Maybe we can set aside time each week for self-care and make sure we communicate openly about how we're feeling."

Rufina: "That sounds like a good plan. We can also investigate couples therapy to help us navigate this together."

Conversation 3: Considering Mental Health Before Marriage

Niraj: "Priya, before we get married, it is important we talk about our mental health. I want us to be prepared for any challenges."

Priya: "I agree, Niraj. I have had depression in the past, and it is important you know about it."

Niraj: "Thank you for sharing that with me. I have had my struggles with anxiety, too. Maybe we can see a counsellor together to make sure we're on the same page."

Priya: "that is a great idea. I want us to have a solid foundation for our future."

Activity: Reflect and Act

1. **Reflection:** Take some time to reflect on your own mental health and how it affects your relationship. Write down your thoughts and discuss them with your partner.

2. **Action:** Plan a self-care day for both you and your partner. This could include activities like meditation, exercise, or simply spending quality time together without distractions. Join a support group that helps you as well as your partner. Self-care will help you from burnout and fallout as well.

3. **Mental Health Check-In:** Schedule regular mental health check-ins to discuss feelings, concerns, and progress. This helps maintain

open communication and provides ongoing support.

Check-In Questions:

How have you been feeling emotionally and mentally?

Are there any specific stressors or challenges you are facing?

How can I support you better in managing your mental health?

Self-Reflections

1. **Personal Boundaries:** Reflect on what boundaries you need to set to protect your mental health. Write them down and discuss them with your partner.

2. **Support Systems:** Identify the people and resources you can turn to for support. This might include friends, family, support groups, or professional counsellors.

3. **Future Planning:** Think about your long-term goals and how mental health might impact them. Discuss these with your partner to ensure you are both aligned.

Conclusion

Addressing mental health in relationships is essential for building a strong, supportive partnership. Open communication, empathy, and professional support can help couples navigate the challenges of mental health issues. By being forthcoming and honest about mental health, couples can create a foundation of trust and understanding, ensuring a healthier and more resilient relationship.

References

- American Psychological Association (APA) discusses the importance of relationships in mental health and well-being4.

- National Association of School Psychologists (NASP) highlights the link between mental health and overall life outcomes5.

- Harvard Health emphasizes the impact of healthy relationships on mental and physical health6.

- Psychology Today provides insights into the importance of discussing mental health before marriage.

- Verywell Health outlines the benefits of premarital counselling in addressing mental health issues.

- Corrigan, P. W., Druss, B. G., & Perlick, D. A. (2014). The impact of mental illness stigma on seeking and participating in mental health care. Psychological

Science in the Public Interest, 15(2), 37-70.

- Gottman, J. M., & Silver, N. (2015). The seven principles for making marriage work. New York: Harmony Books.

- Kessler, R. C., Berglund, P., Demler, O., Jin, R., Merikangas, K. R., & Walters, E. E. (2005). Lifetime prevalence and age-of-onset distributions of DSM-IV disorders in the National Comorbidity Survey Replication. Archives of General Psychiatry, 62(6), 593-602.

- Reupert, A., & Maybery, D. (2010). "Knowledge is power": Educating children about their parent's mental illness. Social Work in Health Care, 49(7), 630-646.

- Sharf, R. S. (2015). Theories of psychotherapy and counselling: Concepts and cases (6th ed.). Belmont, CA: Brooks/Cole.

Chapter 4

Navigating Loss Together: Supporting Your Partner Through Grief

The loss of a parent, sibling, or dear friend can be one of the most challenging experiences in life. This chapter offers guidance on how couples can navigate the grieving process together. It explores the importance of empathy, communication, and support as partners face loss and find ways to heal. Through meaningful dialogue, reflective practices, and supportive activities, couples can strengthen their bond and help each other through the grief journey.

"Grief is the price we pay for love." — *Queen Elizabeth II*

In the shadow of loss, hand in hand, we tread,
Through sorrow's path, by love, we are led.
In hearts entwined, together we mend,
In grief and love, we find our trend.

Introduction

The loss of a loved one is a profound experience that shakes the very foundation of our lives. When a partner faces the grief of losing a parent, sibling, or dear friend, it can be challenging to know how to offer support. This chapter delves into the conversations and actions couples can take to navigate the complex emotions of grief together. By fostering empathy, open communication, and mutual support, couples can find strength in their partnership and begin the healing process.

Understanding Grief:

Grief manifests in myriad ways, from deep sadness and anger to confusion and numbness. Understanding that grief is a deeply personal and unique journey is crucial. Each person experiences and processes loss differently and recognizing these differences can help partners offer the right support.

I vividly remember 18 years ago when I lost my dearest sister in Australia. It was a heart-wrenching time, and sitting in church at her funeral was one of the biggest challenges I faced. I was inconsolable. Throughout the service, my sadness, feelings of deep loss, and unbearable grief were expressed by unceasing sobbing. I tried to muffle my sobbing, but it only got worse, especially when the photos were shown. I almost wanted to run to the casket where my sister lay and hug her, never letting her go.

Amidst this overwhelming sorrow, my husband quietly put his arm around me and, without saying a word, squeezed my hand in silence and understanding. It was at that moment that someone understood my pain. Miraculously, my crying ceased, and tears were shed, but silently. Such is the profound role of a partner: to be there when your spouse is going through the pangs of pain for the loss of their beloved family member or best friend.

A partner's silent support can be the anchor that helps one navigate through the storm of grief. Their presence alone, without the need for words, speaks volumes. It is about being there, providing comfort, and allowing the grieving person to express their sorrow in their own way. Whether through a gentle touch, a quiet hug, or simply sitting beside them in silence, these gestures can make an immeasurable difference.

Recognizing the uniqueness of each person's grief journey enables partners to offer the right kind of support. It is not about having the perfect words to say but about being present and showing empathy. Understanding that grief does not have a timeline and allowing space for the various emotions that come with it is essential. The strength of a relationship often shines through in these moments, proving that love and support can help heal even the deepest wounds.

Dialogue:

- **Bren:** "I'm struggling with the loss of my brother. I don't even know how to feel because I could not even go to the funeral; we had just come here a month ago."

- **Val:** "I'm here for you. It is okay to feel whatever you are feeling. Let us take it one day at a time and know that we spent quality time with him, when we were with him. You gave him not just your time but help in so many other ways. You have loved him so dearly honey."

Communicating Effectively: Open and honest communication is vital when navigating grief. Encourage your partner to share their feelings and listen without judgment. Providing a safe space for expression can significantly aid the healing process.

Dialogue:

- Bren: "I'm feeling overwhelmed and truly miserable that he was so alone in life, especially when we migrated. It must have really made him feel lost and lonely."

- Val: "Yes, loneliness is such a sad illness. It is probably that he lost hope and his best friend. It is a pity we cannot delay our arrival because our children are starting their school term here. I can imagine the guilt you are going through; however, remember, it is not your fault; we could not have stopped whatever he was going through. His heart attack could have been more from a combination of so many things he lost in life. He died of a broken heart syndrome and extreme sadness. Try to pray for his soul."

Offering Practical Support: Practical help can be immensely beneficial besides emotional support. Whether handling daily chores, making meals, or arranging memorial services, taking on responsibilities can relieve some of the burden from your grieving partner.

Example Dialogue:

- Bren: "I can't keep up with everything right now."

- Val: "Let me take care of the household tasks for a while. You need to rest and process your feelings."

Honouring the Loved One's Memory: Finding ways to honour and remember the deceased can be a healing practice. Engage in rituals or activities that commemorate their life and the impact they had.

Dialogue:

- Bren: "I miss him so much. I want to do something to remember him."

- Val: "How about we create a photo album or a memory box together? It could be a unique way to keep their memory alive. Also, check out this photo frame of your brother. I had it laminated for. We can put it in our house and remember him when he was alive and always smile. "

- Bret: "Thanks, Val. This is absolutely beautiful of you and thanks so much for helping me through my grieving process. You have been so wonderful to talk, and always ready to lend your shoulder to cry, and allowing me to speak about my brother every time I wanted to. Thanks for organizing the prayer service for him too. He is in a better resting place".

Activity

Creating a Memory Box: Together, create a memory box where you can keep mementos, photos, and letters that remind you of the loved one. This activity can be a therapeutic way to honour their memory and process their grief.

Steps:

1. Find a suitable box that can be decorated.

2. Collect items that remind you of the loved one.

3. Write letters or notes about your memories and feelings.

4. Place the items and letters in the box.

5. Take time to go through the box together, sharing stories and memories.

Self-Reflection

Reflective Journaling: Encourage each partner to keep a journal to reflect on their feelings and experiences. Writing can be a powerful way to process emotions and gain insight into grieving.

Example Journal Prompts:

- What are your most cherished memories of the loved one?

- How has the loss affected you emotionally and mentally?

- What can you do to honour their memory and find peace?

Dialogue

Supporting Conversations:

- Bren: "I think of him so much more than before."

- Val: "Of course you do. He was not just your brother but your best friend, too. You had so much fun together. I remember how you got him all the clothes, watches, and belts from your trips abroad."

- Bren: "Thank you for reminding me of that. Yes, I loved him so very much. It's such a pity that his family deserted him."

- Val: "We're doing this together. Let us take it one step at a time and lean on each other. I am sure you would do the same for me."

Conclusion

Navigating the loss of a loved one is a deeply personal yet challenging journey. By fostering empathy, open communication, and mutual support, couples can help each other through the grieving process. Remembering the loved one together and finding ways to honour their memory can also be powerful steps toward healing. Through love and compassion, couples can emerge stronger and more connected as they move forward together.

References

1. Bonanno, G. A. (2009). The other side of sadness: What the new science of bereavement tells us about life after loss. Basic Books.

2. Stroebe, M. S., Hansson, R. O., Schut, H., & Stroebe, W. (2008). Handbook of bereavement research and practice: Advances in theory and intervention. American Psychological Association.

3. Worden, J. W. (2009). Grief counseling and grief therapy: A handbook for the mental health practitioner. Springer Publishing Company.

4. Neimeyer, R. A. (2016). Techniques of grief therapy: Creative practices for counseling the bereaved. Routledge.

5. Silverman, P. R., & Kelly, M. (2009). A parent's guide to raising grieving children: Rebuilding your family after the death of a loved one. Oxford University Press.

Chapter 5

Breaking the Silence: Understanding and Addressing Domestic Violence

This chapter explores the critical issue of domestic violence, providing a comprehensive understanding of its impact on individuals and relationships. It offers practical strategies for identifying, addressing, and overcoming domestic violence, emphasizing the importance of safety, support, and healing.

"The first step towards ending the cycle of violence is breaking the silence and seeking help. No one deserves to live in fear." – Unknown

> *In the quiet of the night, voices often fade,*
>
> *But the echoes of fear remain, in hearts they invade.*
>
> *Strength is found in whispers, in reaching out for aid,*
>
> *Together we can break the chains, in courage unafraid.*

Introduction:

Domestic violence is a pervasive issue that affects millions of individuals worldwide, transcending socioeconomic status, culture, and gender. In Australia alone, an estimated **4.2 million adults (21%)** have experienced violence, emotional abuse, or economic abuse by a partner. Tragically, domestic violence has led to numerous deaths and long-lasting trauma. Disturbingly, the risk of homicide increases significantly when a partner leaves the relationship, making it imperative to approach this issue with utmost care.

It has become crucial to educate all members of society about domestic violence to recognize the signs early and intervene before it escalates. This education is especially important within LGBTQ+ relationships, where additional challenges and complexities may arise. Ensuring safety and providing support are paramount, and conversations about domestic violence should happen with trusted family members and friends only.

Statistics:

- **1 in 5 Australians** have experienced partner violence or abuse.

- **11.3% of Australian adults** have experienced violence from a partner (current or previous cohabiting).

- Domestic violence costs Australia **$21.7 billion annually in health,** social services, and lost productivity.

Strategies to Stay Safe:

1. **Recognize the Signs:** Be aware of the early signs of abuse, such as controlling behaviour, jealousy, and isolation.

2. **Create a Safety Plan:** Identify safe places to go in an emergency, list important phone numbers, and pack an emergency bag with essential items.

3. **Seek Help:** Reach out to domestic violence hotlines, shelters, and support groups for assistance and guidance.

4. **Educate Yourself and Others:** Learn about domestic violence and share this knowledge with friends, family, and your community to raise awareness.

5. **Foster Healthy Relationships:** Promote respect, communication, and equality in all relationships.

6. **Converse with Trusted Family Members Only:** Ensure that discussions about your situation are held with family members and friends who can be trusted to provide support and keep your safety as a priority.

By understanding the signs, fostering open communication, and providing support, we can create a safer and more compassionate world. Remember, no one deserves to live in fear, and there is always help available. Together, we can influence and support survivors in their journey towards healing and recovery.

By understanding the signs, fostering open communication, and providing support, we can create a safer and more compassionate world.

Remember, no one deserves to live in fear, and there is always help available. Together, we can be effective and support survivors in their journey towards healing and recovery.

Understanding Domestic Violence:

Breaking the Silence: Understanding and Addressing Domestic Violence

When Diane met Henry, everything seemed perfect. Their love story began like many others, filled with joy, laughter, and shared dreams. But behind closed doors, Diane's reality slowly started to shift. The once gentle words turned sharp, the loving touch became controlling, and Diane found herself trapped in a cycle of fear and confusion.

Recognizing the Signs and Patterns of Abuse

Diane had heard about domestic violence but never imagined it could happen to her. She was in denial at first, making excuses for Henry's behaviour. But as the instances of physical, emotional, and psychological abuse escalated, she could not ignore the signs any longer. The bruises, the isolation from friends and family, and the constant fear of making a wrong move were all red flags.

The Impact of Domestic Violence

The impact of Henry's abuse on Diane was profound. She found herself constantly anxious, her self-esteem eroding with every passing day. She felt trapped, unable to break free from the cycle of violence. The toll on her physical health was evident, with frequent injuries and chronic stress affecting her well-being. The impact extended to their children, who were caught in the crossfire, witnessing the violence and experiencing their own trauma.

Taking the First Step: Creating a Safety Plan

One evening, after a particularly violent incident, Diane knew she had to act. She secretly reached out to a local domestic violence hotline. The counsellor at the other end of the line provided her with the support and resources she needed. Together, they created a safety plan. Diane identified a safe place to go in an emergency and packed an emergency bag with essential items. She listed important phone numbers, including the hotline, trusted friends, and shelters.

Seeking Help: Finding Support Systems

Diane's journey to safety was not easy. With the help of the hotline counsellor, she found a shelter where she and her children could stay temporarily. The shelter provided a safe haven and connected her with legal aid to explore her options for restraining orders and custody arrangements.

Diane also started attending support group meetings where she met others who had faced similar situations. Sharing her story and hearing others' experiences gave her strength and hope.

Healing and Recovery

Healing was a gradual process. Diane began attending therapy sessions to work through the trauma and rebuild her self-esteem. She focused on self-care, nurturing her physical and emotional health. Over time, she started to reclaim her sense of identity and independence. Her children, too, benefited from counselling, helping them process their experiences and heal from the emotional scars.

Offering Support to Others: Diane's Conversation with Sarah

A year later, Diane encountered Sarah, a friend who was showing signs of being in an abusive relationship. Diane approached her gently, "I've noticed some changes in your behaviour lately, and I'm really concerned. Is everything okay at home?" Sarah hesitated but eventually opened up. Diane listened attentively, sharing her own story, and encouraging Sarah to seek help. "You're not alone, Sarah. There are people who can help you, just like they helped me."

Actual Conversations:

1. **Starting the Conversation:**

   o   Partner A: "I've noticed some changes in your behaviour lately, and I'm really concerned. Is everything okay at home?"

   o   Partner B: (hesitant) "It's been tough...I don't know how to talk about it."

2. **Offering Support:**

   o   Friend: "I want you to know that I'm here for you, no matter what. You don't have to go through this alone."

   o   Victim: "Thank you. It's hard to talk about, but I need help."

3. **Seeking Professional Help:**

   o   Counsellor: "Your safety is our top priority. Let's work on a safety plan together and explore the resources available to you."

   o   Victim: "I'm scared, but I know I need to take these steps for myself and my children."

Activity: Create a Safety Plan

•   Identify a safe place to go in an emergency.

- List important phone numbers (hotlines, trusted friends or family, shelters).
- Pack an emergency bag with essential items (clothes, medications, important documents).
- Plan and practice an escape route.

Reflection: Take some time to reflect on the importance of addressing domestic violence. Write about what you have learned from this chapter, how you can support someone experiencing domestic violence, and what steps you can take to raise awareness in your community.

Reflection Activity

Take some time to reflect on what you have learned from Diane's story. Write about how you can support someone experiencing domestic violence and what steps you can take to raise awareness in your community. Consider creating a safety plan for yourself or someone you know who may be in an analogous situation.

Conclusion

Diane's story is a testament to the importance of breaking the silence around domestic violence. By recognizing the signs, seeking help, and fostering a supportive community, we can create a safer world for everyone. Remember, no one deserves to live in fear. There is always help available, and together, we can have influence.

Breaking the silence around domestic violence is a critical step towards ending its cycle. By understanding the signs, providing support, and fostering open communication, we can create a safer and more compassionate world. Remember, no one deserves to live in fear, and there is always help available. Together, we can be effective and support survivors in their journey towards healing and recovery.

Academic References:

1. Black, M. C., Basile, K. C., Breiding, M. J., Smith, S. G., Walters, M. L., Merrick, M. T., ... & Stevens, M. R. (2011). The National Intimate Partner and Sexual Violence Survey (NISVS): 2010 summary report. National Center for Injury Prevention and Control, Centres for Disease Control and Prevention.

2. Campbell, J. C. (2002). Health consequences of intimate partner violence. The Lancet, 359(9314), 1331-1336.

3. Heise, L. L., & García-Moreno, C. (2002). Violence by intimate partners. World Report on Violence and Health, 87-121.

4. Stark, E. (2007). Coercive control: The entrapment of women in personal life.

Oxford University Press.

5. World Health Organization. (2013). Global and regional estimates of violence against women: prevalence and health effects of intimate partner violence and non-partner sexual violence. World Health Organization.

Module 5
Farewell with Dignity: Navigating Breakup Discussions

goodbye

Chapter 1

Honouring the End: Navigating Conversations about Ending the Relationship

Ending a relationship is a painful and complex process that requires sensitivity, honesty, and respect. This chapter explores how to approach these difficult conversations with empathy and care. Learn strategies for initiating the conversation, managing emotional reactions, and navigating the practical aspects of separation. By managing the end of a relationship with dignity and compassion, both partners can find closure and begin the healing process.

Quote: *"Every new beginning comes from some other beginning's end."* — *Seneca*

In the quiet of goodbye, hearts may ache,

Yet through the tears, new paths we'll make.

With kindness and grace, we part our ways,

Honouring love that once set our hearts ablaze.

Introduction:

Ending a relationship is one of the most challenging experiences individuals can face. It involves a whirlwind of emotions, from sadness and anger to relief and hope. Navigating these conversations requires a delicate balance of honesty and empathy, ensuring that both partners feel heard and respected.

This chapter provides a comprehensive guide for having these difficult conversations. We will explore practical strategies for initiating the breakup talk, managing emotional reactions, and addressing the logistical aspects of separation. By approaching the end of a relationship with dignity and compassion, both partners can find a path toward healing and new beginnings.

149

Recognizing the Signs When the End is Nigh

Persistent Unhappiness: One of the clearest signs that a relationship might be nearing its end is persistent unhappiness. When joy and contentment are replaced by constant dissatisfaction and unhappiness, it may be time to evaluate the future of the relationship.

Lack of Communication: Communication is the foundation of any healthy relationship. When partners stop communicating openly and honestly, and conversations become shallow or non-existent, it indicates a significant breakdown in the connection.

Frequent Conflicts: While disagreements are normal, constant arguments and unresolved conflicts can signal deeper issues. If conflicts become the norm rather than the exception, it might be time to reconsider the relationship.

Emotional Detachment: When one or both partners become emotionally detached and indifferent, it signifies a loss of intimacy and connection. This detachment can manifest as a lack of interest in each other's lives and feelings.

Loss of Trust: Trust is vital for a healthy relationship. If trust has been broken and cannot be rebuilt, it erodes the foundation of the relationship, making it difficult to move forward together.

Ending a Relationship, the Right Way

Prepare for the Conversation: Before initiating the breakup conversation, take time to reflect on your feelings and the reasons for ending the relationship. Be clear and honest with yourself about why you feel it's time to part ways.

The Importance of a Compassionate Approach

Emotional Closure: Providing emotional closure is crucial for both partners. Honest and respectful conversations help individuals understand the reasons for the breakup and begin the healing process.

Respecting Each Other: Ending a relationship with respect and kindness helps maintain dignity for both parties. It reduces the likelihood of lingering resentment and promotes a sense of closure.

Clear Communication: Clear and direct communication minimizes misunderstandings. It ensures that both partners are aware of the reasons for the breakup and can process the information with clarity.

Activities and Exercises

Activity: Reflective Journaling: Encourage each partner to maintain a reflective journal during this process. Writing down thoughts and feelings can help with emotional processing and provide clarity.

Dialogue:

- Nerissa: "I've been reflecting on our relationship and think it's time for an honest conversation about where we're heading."

- Samir: "I appreciate your honesty. Let's talk about it."

Choose the Right Time and Place: Select a private, quiet setting where both partners can speak openly without interruption.   Ensure you have enough time for a thorough discussion.

Dialogue:

- Nerissa: "Can we find a private place to talk about something important?"

- Samir: "Sure, let's sit down somewhere quiet. How about we go to the park?"

Be Honest and Compassionate: Communicate your feelings honestly but with kindness. Avoid blaming or criticizing your partner; instead, focus on your own experiences and emotions.

Dialogue:

- Nerissa: "I've felt unhappy and disconnected for a while now. It's important   to me that we part ways respectfully."

- Samir: "Thank you for being honest. This is hard to hear, but I respect your feelings. I am so sorry if you have felt neglected or hurt. Can we work on this relationship for the sake of our children?"

Allow Space for Emotions: Understand that both partners will experience a range of emotions. Allow space for these feelings and offer support, even if it's just listening.

Dialogue:

- Nerissa: "I know this is painful. It is okay to feel upset and emotional. However, in the last 6 months, I have developed feelings for someone else, and I cannot turn back."

- Samir: " This is really tough for me; I trusted you implicitly and cannot even fathom when I became obsolete for you."

- Nerissa: "Well, without planting the entire blame on you, I was unhappy for a long time and kept it to myself and then when I met this person, I felt re-energized, and without realizing it, I found myself giving permission to explore the new relationship. I am extremely sorry to have hurt you. However, my mind is made up, and it is difficult to turn back now" I hope you can respect my honesty and allow me the freedom to choose.

- Samir: "I know I have always respected your wishes, and even though this is excruciatingly painful and horrendous for me, I will allow you time to think".

Discuss Practical Matters: Address the logistical aspects of the breakup, such as living arrangements, shared responsibilities, and financial matters.

Dialogue:

- Nerissa: "I have been giving it a lot of thought and have already made a decision. Help me make this easy, and whenever you are ready, we will discuss our next move, about moving out, finances, etc."

- Samir: "Well, I can see, I really have no choice, and despite me reeling with shock, let's talk about this another time."

- Nerissa: "I am very sorry dear; however, I need to be honest with myself".

Activities for Couples Considering Ending the Relationship

Activity: Reflective Journaling: Encourage each partner to maintain a reflective journal. Writing down thoughts and feelings can help with emotional processing and provide clarity.

Example Journal Prompts:

- What are my main emotions about potentially ending this relationship?

- What do I need to heal and move forward?

- What have I learned from this relationship that I can take into future relationships?

Exercise: Support System Mapping: Create a map of your support system, identifying friends, family, and resources that can provide emotional support during this transition.

Mapping Questions:

- Who can I reach out to for emotional support?

- What activities or practices help me cope with stress and sadness?

- How can I create a routine that supports my well-being?

Activity: Professional counselling: Consider seeking the help of a professional counsellor or therapist. A neutral third party can offer guidance and support as you navigate these problematic decisions.

Dialogue:

- Samir: "I think it might help if we see a counsellor to discuss our issues".

- Nerissa: "I agree. It could provide us with some clarity and support."

Reflective Practice

Self-Reflection and Growth: Engage in regular self-reflection to understand your emotions and growth during this transition. Reflect on what you have learned about yourself and your needs.

Reflection Prompts:

- How have I grown through this relationship and its ending?

- What are my core values and needs in a relationship?

- How can I use this experience to build healthier relationships in the future?

Conclusion

Ending a relationship with compassion and respect allows both partners to find closure and begin the healing process. By recognizing the signs when the relationship is ending, communicating openly, and overseeing practical matters thoughtfully, couples can navigate this difficult transition with dignity. While the end of a relationship is painful, it also offers an opportunity for personal growth and new beginnings.

References

- Amato, P. R. (2010). Research on divorce: Continuing trends and new developments. Journal of Marriage and Family, 72(3), 650-666.

- Hetherington, E. M., & Kelly, J. (2002). For better or for worse: Divorce reconsidered. New York: W.W. Norton & Company.

- Rollie, S. S., & Duck, S. (2006). Divorce and dissolution of romantic relationships: Stage models and their limitations. In M. A. Fine & J. H. Harvey

(Eds.), Handbook of divorce and relationship dissolution (pp. 223-240). Mahwah, NJ: Lawrence Erlbaum Associates.

- Sbarra, D. A., & Emery, R. E. (2005). The emotional sequelae of nonmarital relationship dissolution: Analysis of change and intraindividual variability over time. Personal Relationships, 12(2), 213-232.

- Tashiro, T., & Frazier, P. (2003). "I'll never be in a relationship like that again": Personal growth following romantic relationship breakups. Personal Relationships, 10(1), 113-128

Chapter 2

Financial Fairness: Dividing Finances Amiably

Dividing finances is a critical step in navigating the end of a relationship and managing it amiably can make a significant difference in the process. This chapter provides strategies for fair and transparent financial separation, ensuring both partners feel respected and secure. Learn how to approach financial conversations, document assets and liabilities, and negotiate a settlement that considers both parties' needs and future well-being.

"Good financial decisions are critical to creating a secure future, particularly during transitions." — Suze Orman

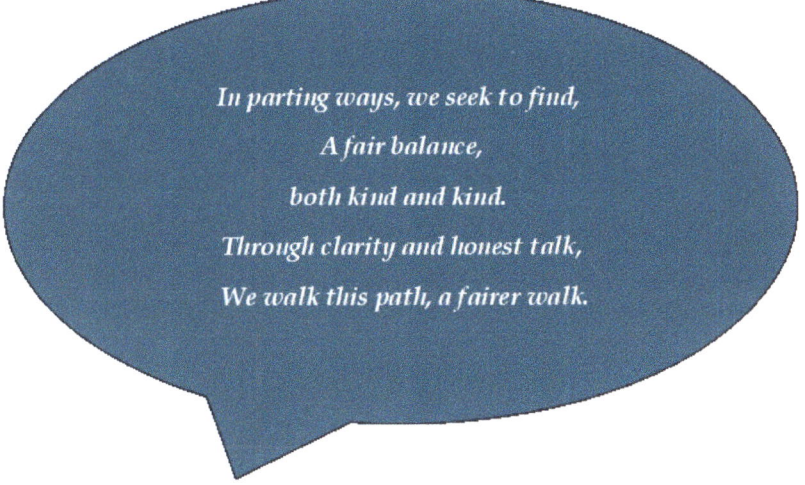

In parting ways, we seek to find,

A fair balance,

both kind and kind.

Through clarity and honest talk,

We walk this path, a fairer walk.

Introduction:

Financial matters often intensify the complexities of ending a relationship. A fair and transparent approach to dividing finances can ease the transition and promote a sense of closure and security for both partners. Addressing finances amiably involves clear communication, equitable division of assets and debts, and a focus on future stability.

Dividing finances into a relationship can be a delicate topic, but with open communication and mutual respect, it can be managed amiably. This chapter explores effective strategies for navigating financial separation, including documenting assets and liabilities, negotiating settlements, and seeking professional guidance. By approaching these conversations with honesty and mutual respect, couples can achieve a fair financial resolution that supports their individual paths forward.

Here are some strategies and tips to help couples navigate this important aspect of their relationship:

Recognizing the Importance of Fair Financial Division

When Karla and Dan decided to separate, they understood that fair financial division would be crucial to reduce potential conflicts and help them move forward with a sense of justice and respect. One evening, they sat down with a cup of tea and initiated transparent discussions about their finances. They knew that openly discussing their financial goals and concerns would prevent misunderstandings and foster cooperation.

Reducing Conflict

As they talked, Karla expressed her worries about potential conflicts over money. "I don't want us to fight over finances," she admitted. Dan nodded in agreement, "Neither do I. Let's make sure we manage this fairly so we can both move on without resentment." By acknowledging the importance of equitable division, they set the stage for a smoother separation process.

Ensuring Financial Stability

Karla and Dan worked together to ensure that both partners would maintain financial stability after the separation. They listed all their assets and liabilities, discussing how to divide them equitably. "We need to make sure neither of us is left with a disproportionate financial burden," Dan emphasized. This approach helped them support each other's future well-being, avoiding any unfair financial strain.

Promoting Emotional Healing

Addressing their financial matters with compassion and fairness allowed Karla and Dan to focus on their emotional recovery. Karla remarked, "Knowing we're managing our finances fairly helps reduce my stress." Dan agreed, adding, "It creates a collaborative atmosphere, which makes this difficult process a bit easier." Their amicable financial division promoted emotional healing by reducing stress and fostering a sense of cooperation.

Practical Strategies for Dividing Finances Amiably

To divide their finances amiably, Karla and Dan followed practical strategies, starting with open communication. They initiated financial conversations with honesty and transparency, ensuring mutual understanding. "Let's be upfront with what we have and what we need," Karla suggested. This open dialogue helped them align their financial expectations and find common ground.

By prioritizing fair financial division, Karla and Dan were able to reduce conflicts, ensure financial stability, and promote emotional healing during their separation. Their approach highlighted the importance of compassion, honesty, and cooperation, setting a positive example for navigating the complexities of ending a relationship.

Dialogue:

Samir: "We need to discuss our finances and how to divide them fairly. Can we have an open and honest conversation about our assets and debts?"

Nerissa: "Yes, let's make sure we approach this with transparency and respect."

Documenting Assets and Liabilities: Create a comprehensive list of all assets and liabilities. This includes bank accounts, investments, real estate, loans, and credit card debts. Transparency in documenting these items ensures a fair division.

Dialogue:

Samir: "Let's list all our assets and debts so we can see the full picture."

Nerissa: "Agreed. I have never had or owned much, because I was a full-time Mom for 10 years of my life, so I will leave it up to you to do the right thing."

Negotiating Settlements: Approach negotiations with a focus on fairness and future needs. Consider both partners' financial situations and aim for a settlement that supports both individuals moving forward.

Dialogue:

Nerissa: "How do we divide our assets and debts in a way that feels fair to both of us?"

Samir: "We should consider our current financial needs and future stability. Let's find a balance."

Seeking Professional Guidance: Consider consulting a financial advisor or mediator. Professional guidance can provide an objective perspective and help facilitate fair negotiations.

Dialogue:

Samir: "I think it might help if we consult a financial advisor to ensure we're making informed decisions."

Nerissa: "That's a good idea. Professional advice can help us navigate this process more smoothly."

Activities and Exercises

Activity: Financial Inventory: Create a detailed financial inventory. Document all assets, liabilities, income sources, and expenses. Review this inventory together to ensure accuracy and transparency.

Inventory Items:

Bank accounts and balances.

Investments (stocks, bonds, retirement accounts)

Real estate properties

Loans and credit card debts

Monthly expenses and income

Exercise: Financial Goals Discussion: Discuss your individual financial goals and needs for the future. Understanding each other's priorities helps in negotiating a fair settlement.

Discussion Questions:

What are your immediate financial needs?

What are your long-term financial goals?

How can we divide our assets and debts to support these goals?

Reflective Practice

Self-Reflection and Growth: Reflect on your financial habits and how they have impacted your relationship. Consider how this experience can inform your future financial decisions and relationships.

Reflection Prompts:

How have my financial habits affected our relationship?

What have I learned about managing finances during this process?

How can I apply these lessons to future financial decisions?

Activities and Reflections

- **Activity:** Create a list of all marital assets and classify them as either marital or individual property. Discuss how you would like these assets to be divided in the event of a separation.

- **Reflection:** Reflect on how the well-being of your children would be impacted by the separation of assets. Consider what steps you can take to ensure their needs are met.

Establishing Shared Financial Goals

Meet Anne and Amaro, a couple who recently got married and are eager to start their lives together on the right foot. They knew that discussing their financial aspirations as a couple was crucial. One evening, over a cozy dinner, they sat down to talk about their dreams and goals. "I want us to have a clear vision of our future together," Amaro said. Understanding each other's goals helped them align their financial decisions and create a sense of partnership. They decided to save for a house, plan for vacations, and set aside funds for future family expenses.

Creating a Budget Together

To keep their finances on track, Anne and Amaro worked together to create a budget that reflected both their incomes and expenses. They listed out their monthly earnings, fixed costs like rent and utilities, and variable expenses such as groceries and entertainment. "This way, we can see exactly where our money is going and ensure we're both contributing fairly," Anne noted. The budget became their financial blueprint, helping them manage their spending and avoid unnecessary debt.

Deciding on a Proportional Split

One of the fair ways they decided to divide their finances was to split expenses proportionally based on their incomes. Since Amaro earned 60% of their total household income, he contributed 60% towards shared expenses, while Anne covered the remaining 40%. "This method feels fair and reflects our financial capacities," Anne said, feeling relieved that they found a balanced approach.

Contributing Equally

Alternatively, some couples prefer to split expenses equally, regardless of income. Anne and Amaro considered this option too, especially since their incomes were similar. They decided that for certain expenses like dining out and entertainment, they would split the costs equally. "This keeps things simple and ensures we both feel equally responsible," Amaro added.

Allocating Specific Expenses

To further simplify their monetary management, they decided to assign specific expenses to each partner. Anne took responsibility for paying the rent, while Amaro oversaw groceries and utilities. "Dividing responsibilities this way makes it easier to track our contributions," Anne explained, appreciating the clarity it brought to their financial planning.

Opening a Joint Bank Account

They also considered opening a joint bank account for shared expenses. After discussing the pros and cons, they decided it would make managing bills and tracking spending more convenient. "We'll need to maintain open communication and trust to avoid any conflicts," Amaro emphasized, ensuring they both felt comfortable with this arrangement.

Separate Accounts with Shared Contributions

For other expenses, Anne and Amaro chose to keep their individual bank accounts but contributed to a shared account for joint expenses. This approach allowed them financial independence while ensuring they were both contributing to the household. "It's the best of both worlds," Anne said, feeling confident in their financial system.

Using Expense-Splitting Apps or Tools

To manage their shared expenses and ensure transparency, they explored various apps and tools designed for couples. These digital aids helped them track spending and split costs effortlessly, avoiding any potential misunderstandings.

Legal Implications and Separation of Assets When One Person Has Custody of All Children

When Anna and Amaro faced the difficult decision to separate, the legal implications and separation of assets became complex, especially since Anna had custody of their children. Understanding these implications was crucial for ensuring a fair and equitable division of assets and providing for the well-being of the children.

Legal Implications - Best Interests of the Child

The court prioritized the best interests of their children when making custody decisions. Factors considered included the children's physical and emotional needs, stability, and the ability of each parent to provide a safe and nurturing environment.

Child Support

Amaro was required to pay child support to Anna, as the custodial parent. The amount was determined based on their incomes, the needs of the children, and the standard of living the children would have enjoyed if the marriage had not ended. "It's important that the kids' needs are met," Amaro acknowledged.

Spousal Support

In some cases, Anne was also entitled to spousal support (alimony) to help maintain her standard of living and support the children. "This will help me manage our expenses while focusing on the kids," Anna said.

Legal Representation

Both Anne and Amaro sought legal representation to navigate the complexities of custody and asset division. Their divorce lawyers ensured that all assets were disclosed and divided fairly, providing guidance throughout the process.

Separation of Assets

Marital vs. Individual Property

They learned that assets are classified as either marital or individual property. Marital property included assets acquired during the marriage, while individual property encompassed assets owned before the marriage or received as gifts or inheritances.

Equitable Distribution

The court aimed for an equitable distribution of marital assets, which may not always be a 50-50 split. Factors considered included the duration of the marriage, the financial status of each spouse, and future earnings prospects. "It's about fairness, not just equal division," their lawyer explained.

Hidden Assets

During the proceedings, they had to ensure that no assets were hidden. Divorce attorneys collaborated with financial specialists to uncover any concealed assets, ensuring a fair division.

Custodial Parent Considerations

Since Anne had custody of the children, the court awarded her a larger share of the marital assets to ensure the children's needs were met. "This will help us maintain stability for the kids," Anne said, feeling reassured by the court's decision.

Get It in Writing: Ensure that all agreements are documented. This includes creating a new budget, making a fair division of accrued items (such as furniture, appliances, and electronics), closing shared accounts, filing for legal separation, and dividing assets1.

Close Joint Bank Accounts: If you do not already have one, open your own bank account. Establish a record of every bank account in existence and divide the shared ones.

Credit Cards and Loans: Obtain a copy of your credit report to identify all the credit cards and loans attached to both spouses. Close any joint credit lines.

Living in the Family Home: Establish a new budget and come to a civil agreement on who should pay what after your separation. All property acquired during your marriage is usually considered marital property by law.

Selling the Marital Home: If you cannot come to terms on sharing the financial responsibility for the mortgage, taxes, and other bills, it may be in your best interest to sell the home and split the profits.

Community vs. Separate Property: Understand how your state views property ownership in a marriage. Community property includes any possessions gained during the marriage, while separate property allows a spouse to remain in control of their original assets.

Discuss Responsibility: Discuss how you will manage your finances and divide monies during your separation. This includes deciding how to split up joint accounts and debts or divvying up who pays what bills.

These steps can help make the process of splitting finances during separation more manageable and less stressful. If you need more detailed guidance, consulting a financial advisor or legal professional is recommended.

Take some time to reflect on your financial habits and discuss them with your partner. Consider the following questions:

- What are your financial goals as a couple?
- How do you currently manage your finances?
- What changes can you make to improve your economic management?

By approaching financial discussions with empathy and understanding, couples can create a harmonious financial partnership that supports their shared goals and strengthens their relationship.

Conclusion

Dividing finances amicably is a critical step in the process of ending a relationship. By approaching financial conversations with honesty, transparency, and mutual   respect, couples can achieve a fair and equitable settlement that supports their individual futures. This collaborative approach not only ensures financial stability   but also promotes emotional healing and closure.

References

- Amato, P. R. (2010). Research on divorce: Continuing trends and new developments. Journal of Marriage and Family, 72(3), 650-666.

- Hetherington, E. M., & Kelly, J. (2002). For better or for worse: Divorce reconsidered. New York: W.W. Norton & Company.

- Rollie, S. S., & Duck, S. (2006). Divorce and dissolution of romantic relationships: Stage models and their limitations. In M. A. Fine & J. H. Harvey (Eds.), Handbook of divorce and relationship dissolution (pp. 223-240). Mahwah, NJ: Lawrence Erlbaum Associates.

- Sbarra, D. A., & Emery, R. E. (2005). The emotional sequelae of nonmarital relationship dissolution: Analysis of change and intraindividual variability over time. Personal Relationships, 12(2), 213-232.

- Tashiro, T., & Frazier, P. (2003). "I'll never be in a relationship like that again": Personal growth following romantic relationship breakups. Personal Relationships, 10(1), 113-128.

- Hagerman, A. (2022). Why Splitting Bills Based on Income Is Best. Retrieved by Adam Hagerman.

- SoFi. (2023). How to Split Finances as a Couple. Retrieved from SoFi.

- Lake, R. (2024). How Parents' Finances Impact Custody Battles. Investopedia. Retrieved from Investopedia.

- Gates, E. (2024). The Role of a Divorce Lawyer in Asset Division and Child Custody Disputes. AJS. Retrieved from AJS.

Chapter 3

Healing Hearts: Resolving Emotional Pain and Dilemmas

Resolving emotional pain and dilemmas in a relationship is an intricate process that requires patience, empathy, and open communication. This chapter explores strategies for addressing and healing emotional wounds, fostering understanding, and rebuilding trust. By navigating these difficult conversations with compassion and clarity, couples can move towards healing and strengthen their connection.

"Sometimes, two people must fall apart to realize how much they need to fall back together." "Healing takes courage, and we all have courage, even if we have to dig a little to find it." — Tori Amos

In the shadow of pain, our hearts seek light,
Through tears and words, we find our might.
With open hearts and hands entwined,
We heal the wounds, and our love is redefined.

Introduction:

Emotional pain and dilemmas are inevitable in any relationship. Whether stemming from misunderstandings, unmet expectations, or deeper issues, addressing these emotional wounds is crucial for maintaining a healthy connection. This chapter provides a roadmap for couples to navigate the challenging terrain of emotional healing. By fostering open communication, empathy, and mutual support, partners can resolve conflicts, rebuild trust, and emerge stronger together.

Separation and divorce can be one of the most challenging and emotionally draining experiences for individuals. The emotional pain and dilemma that arise during this period can be overwhelming. However, having conscious conversations about these feelings can help partners navigate this grim time with empathy and understanding.

Recognizing Emotional Pain and Dilemmas

When Zenia and Zachary decided to part ways, they knew it would not be easy. The emotional pain they both felt was overwhelming, filled with loss, anger, confusion, and anxiety. Recognizing these emotions and understanding their root causes was the first step towards healing.

Acknowledging the Emotional Pain

Both Zenia and Zachary took the time to acknowledge and validate each other's feelings. Zenia expressed, "I feel so lost and hurt right now." Zachary, in turn, shared his own feelings, "I'm angry and confused too." They allowed themselves to grieve and process these emotions, understanding that this was essential for their healing.

Seeking Support

Realizing they could not navigate this journey alone, Zenia and Zachary sought support from friends, family, and support groups. Zenia found solace in talking to her sister, who had been through a similar experience. "It's comforting to share with someone who understands," she said. Zachary, on the other hand, joined a support group for separated partners, finding strength in the shared experiences. They both also sought professional help, seeing a therapist who provided new tools and perspectives to manage their emotional turmoil.

Prioritizing Self-Care

Taking care of themselves physically and emotionally became a priority for both Zenia and Zachary. Zenia focused on her health by eating well, exercising, and getting enough sleep. "I need to take care of myself to feel better," she realized. Zachary engaged in self-care activities that brought him joy and relaxation, such as hiking and painting. These efforts significantly improved their overall well-being.

Communicating Effectively

Clear and respectful communication with each other was essential, especially since they had children to be co-parents. They emphasized the importance of avoiding misunderstandings and further emotional pain. "Let's keep our conversations respectful and focus on what's best for the kids," Zachary suggested. By maintaining open lines of communication, they managed to resolve conflicts more effectively.

Focusing on the Future

While it was important to process their past emotions, Zenia and Zachary knew they needed to focus on the future. They set new goals and envisioned a positive future, which provided hope and motivation during this challenging time. Zenia started planning her career advancement, while Zachary accepted new hobbies and activities. "Focusing on what's ahead helps me stay positive," Zenia said.

Legal and Financial Considerations

Seeking legal advice was crucial for both of them to understand their rights and responsibilities. They addressed their financial concerns and planned for the future, which alleviated some of the stress associated with their separation. "Knowing our legal and financial standing gives me a sense of security," Zachary admitted.

Emphasizing Resilience and Growth

They encouraged each other to embrace resilience and personal growth. Zenia reminded herself, "The end of our relationship doesn't define my worth." She used this time for self-discovery and growth, attending workshops and pursuing new interests. Zachary also focused on personal development, reading self-help books, and setting new life goals. "This is an opportunity for us to grow stronger as individuals," Zachary reflected.

By having open and honest conversations about these aspects, Zenia and Zachary were able to navigate their emotional pain and dilemmas with greater understanding and compassion. Their journey was challenging, but through mutual support and a focus on healing, they moved forward with hope and resilience.

Dialogue:

Zachary: "I've been feeling really hurt by our recent arguments. Can we talk about it?"

Zenia: "I'm sorry you feel that way. Let's discuss what's been bothering you."

Understanding the Dilemma: Emotional dilemmas often arise when partners face conflicting needs or values. Understanding these dilemmas requires empathy and a willingness to see the situation from each other's perspective.

Dialogue:

Zachary: "I feel torn between wanting to give you the freedom to leave the relationship and also fighting for the marriage, what do I do."

Zenia: "I understand it's difficult, because the decision is mine. However, it is me that wants out, I love another person and have long clocked out emotionally from you. I think it would not be wise staying together and trying to make it work, for society or the kids. I do believe you will get over it in time."

Practical Strategies for Healing Emotional Pain

Open Communication: Foster a safe environment for open and honest communication. Encourage each other to share feelings and listen actively without judgment.

Dialogue:

Zachary: "I need to express how I've been feeling lately. Can we talk openly without interruption?"

Zenia: "Of course. I am here to listen. Perhaps I am also a bit overwhelmed with what has happened to us after all these years; I too have been hit almost by an avalanche."

Expressing Empathy: Show empathy by validating each other's feelings. Acknowledge the pain and offer support.

Dialogue:

Zenia: "I understand that you're feeling hurt. Your feelings are valid, and I am here for you. All I can say is I am sorry; I did not mean for this to happen. When I did what I did, I did not realize how very painful separating would be for both of us."

Zachary: "Yes indeed, it is one of the most painful things to go through, after years of togetherness and having kids with you. Sometimes, the pain is unbearable. Thank you for understanding. It means a lot to me. This, by far, has been the most grueling experience of my life, and much that I pray and seek what my faults are and thanks for also taking responsibility. At least you know that I never wanted to give up and also sorry for my faults.

Seeking Resolution Together: Work together to find solutions and compromises that address both partners' needs. Focus on rebuilding trust and strengthening the relationship.

Dialogue:

Zenia "Let's find a way to resolve this issue together. What can we do to improve our communication?"

Zachary: "I agree. Maybe we can set aside time each week to discuss our feelings."

Activities and Exercises

Activity: Emotional Check-In: Schedule regular emotional check-ins to discuss feelings, concerns, and progress. Use this time to address any unresolved issues and celebrate improvements.

Check-In Questions:

How have you been feeling emotionally?

Are there any unresolved issues we need to discuss?

What has been working well in our relationship?

Exercise: Active Listening Practice: Practice active listening by taking turns to share feelings while the other partner listens without interruption. Reflect what you have heard to ensure understanding.

Listening Exercise:

Zachary: "I've been feeling overwhelmed with work, and it's affecting our time together."

Zenia: "I hear that you're feeling overwhelmed, and it's impacting our relationship. What can I do to support you?"

Activity: Joint Problem-Solving: Collaborate on finding solutions to emotional dilemmas. Brainstorm together and produce practical steps to address both partners' needs.

1. Calm and Respectful Approach:

Zenia: "I have been unhappy for a long time, and nothing seems to help us improve our relationship. I am sorry to say this, but I have decided that I want a divorce."

Zachary: "I understand. It has been difficult for both of us. Can we discuss how to move forward in a way that minimizes the pain for both of us and our children?"

Expressing Needs and Expectations:

Zenia: "I need a break from this marriage because I am not happy. I would like a trial separation if you would be willing to commit to six months of marriage counselling to see if we can fix our relationship."

Zachary "I am willing to try counselling. Let us set some ground rules for our separation and work on our communication during this time."

Activity: Reflective Journaling

Objective: To help partners process their emotions and gain clarity on their feelings.

Instructions:

1. Set aside 15-20 minutes each day for journaling.

2. Write about your feelings regarding the separation, focusing on both the positive and negative aspects.

3. Reflect on your role in the relationship and what you have learned from it.

4. Consider your hopes and fears for the future, both individually and as co-parents, if applicable.

5. Share your reflections with your partner during a weekly check-in to foster open communication and mutual understanding.

This chapter aims to provide separating partners with tools to navigate their emotional pain and dilemmas, fostering a respectful and constructive dialogue.

Problem-Solving Steps:

Identify the dilemma or issue.

Discuss each partner's perspective and needs.

Brainstorm viable solutions.

Agree on actionable steps and follow up regularly.

Self-Reflection and Growth: Engage in regular self-reflection to understand your emotions and how they impact the relationship. Reflect on what you have learned and how you can apply these insights to foster a healthier connection.

Reflection Prompts:

How have I contributed to the emotional dilemmas in our relationship?

What steps can I take to improve my communication and empathy?

How can I support my partner's emotional well-being?

Conclusion

Healing emotional pain and resolving dilemmas require patience, empathy, and a commitment to open communication. By addressing these issues together, couples can rebuild trust, deepen their connection, and emerge stronger. This journey of emotional healing not only strengthens the relationship but also fosters personal growth and resilience.

References

- Gottman, J. M. (1999). The Seven Principles for Making Marriage Work. New York: Crown Publishers.

- Hendrix, H., & Hunt, H. L. (2005). Getting the Love You Want: A Guide for Couples. New York: St. Martin's Griffin.

- Johnson, S. M. (2008). Hold Me Tight: Seven Conversations for a Lifetime of Love. New York: Little, Brown and Company.

- Leahy, R. L., Tirch, D. D., & Napolitano, L. A. (2011). Emotion Regulation in Couples and Families: Pathways to Dysfunction and Health. Washington, DC: American Psychological Association.

- Tatkin, S. (2016). Wired for Love: How Understanding Your Partner's Brain and Attachment Style Can Help You Defuse Conflict and Build a Secure Relationship. Oakland, CA: New Harbinger Publications.

- Buscho, A. G. (2023). Seven Ways to Cope with Separation or Divorce. Psychology Today. Retrieved from Psychology Today

Chapter 4

Nurturing Souls: The Role of Faith and Spirituality in Parenting

Co-parenting after a separation or divorce requires cooperation, communication, and a focus on the children's well-being. This chapter explores strategies for effective co-parenting, addressing shared challenges and offering practical solutions for maintaining a harmonious relationship. Learn how to create a supportive environment for your children, establish clear boundaries, and navigate the complexities of shared parenting with empathy and respect.

"The best security blanket a child can have is parents who respect each other." — *Jane Blaustone*

In the tapestry of love and care,

Two hearts unite in a child's welfare.
Through challenges faced and paths unknown,

Together, we build a harmonious home.

"Co-parenting is not a competition between two homes. It is a collaboration of parents doing what is best for the kids." - Heather Hetchler

Co-parenting is a collaborative approach to raising children when parents are separated, divorced, or never married. It involves shared responsibilities and decision-making to ensure the well-being of the child. Effective co-parenting requires empathy, patience, and open communication. Co-parenting can be a complex and emotional journey, especially after the dissolution of a romantic relationship. The focus must shift from the past relationship to the present and future needs of the children. Effective co-parenting involves clear communication, mutual respect, and a commitment to providing a stable and loving environment for your children.

This chapter provides a comprehensive guide to navigating the intricacies of co-parenting. We will explore strategies for fostering cooperation, addressing conflicts, and ensuring that children feel supported and loved by both parents. By prioritizing the well-being of the children and working together, co-parents can create a harmonious and nurturing environment.

Key Strategies for Successful Co-Parenting

When Alisha and Rohan decided to part ways, they knew the journey of co-parenting their children would require patience, understanding, and effort. One of the first key strategies they embraced was to let go of past conflicts. They recognized the importance of moving beyond their grievances to focus on their children's best interests. Alisha vented her frustrations to her friends and therapist, ensuring that her emotions were managed away from the children. This approach helped her maintain a supportive environment at home.

Focusing on their children's needs and well-being became their top priority. By putting their children first, Alisha and Rohan created a stable and nurturing environment. They realized that personal grievances should not overshadow the love and care their children needed.

Effective communication was another cornerstone of their co-parenting strategy. They committed clear, concise, and respectful communication, avoiding criticism, blame, and threats. Keeping their conversations businesslike and cooperative helped them resolve issues efficiently. Active listening also played a crucial role in their interactions. They took turns speaking and ensured they understood each other's perspectives, fostering mutual respect and understanding.

Supporting each other as co-parents was vital. Alisha and Rohan recognized and appreciated each other's efforts, using positive reinforcement to strengthen their co-parenting relationship. A simple acknowledgment like, "I appreciate how you oversaw that situation with our child," went a long way in building a cooperative atmosphere.

Recognizing the importance of effective co-parenting, they saw how their cooperation provided emotional stability for their children. Seeing their parents communicate respectfully gave the children a sense of security, knowing both parents were committed to their well-being. Consistency and structure were also crucial. By maintaining consistent parenting approaches, rules, and expectations across both households, Alisha and Rohan reduced confusion and fostered a stable environment.

As role models, Alisha and Rohan demonstrated healthy communication, conflict resolution, and mutual respect. This example sets a positive standard for their children, teaching them valuable lessons in managing relationships. Practical strategies like establishing clear communication, using shared calendars, co-parenting apps, and regular check-ins helped them coordinate schedules and discuss important matters effectively.

Through these efforts, Alisha and Rohan navigated the complexities of co-parenting, ensuring their children thrived in a supportive and loving environment. Their journey highlighted the significance of cooperation, respect, and putting the children's needs first, setting a durable foundation for their family's future.

Communication Tips for Co-Parenting

When Alisha and Rohit decided to be a co-parent after their separation, they knew that effective communication would be vital. They established clear communication guidelines and set boundaries, understanding that this would help prevent misunderstandings and conflicts. "Let's make sure we stick to our guidelines to avoid any unnecessary arguments," Alisha suggested.

They also learned to use "I" statements to express their feelings without blaming each other. "I feel overwhelmed when I don't get updates about the kids' schedules," Rohan would say, promoting constructive dialogue. Maintaining a calm tone was crucial, especially during challenging discussions. "Let's stay calm and respectful, even when things get tough," Alisha reminded me.

Keeping conversations child-focused helped them avoid personal attacks. They always prioritized the needs of their children over their grievances. "Our main focus should be on what's best for the kids," Rohan emphasized. Utilizing technology, they used shared calendars and co-parenting apps to facilitate communication and coordination, making sure their schedules were aligned for visitation and notable events.

Example: Discussing Visitation Schedules

To discuss visitation schedules, they set a meeting with their shared calendar open. "Let's figure out a fair visitation schedule that works for both of us and the kids," Rohan said. They reviewed their commitments and coordinated a plan that ensured both parents had quality time with their children.

Benefits of Positive Co-Parenting

Research shows that children raised by cooperative co-parents have fewer behaviour problems and are closer to their fathers than those raised by hostile co-parents or single parents. Alisha and Rohan realized that effective co-parenting lowered their children's stress and anxiety levels, reduced conflicts between them, and provided stability. "Seeing us working together peacefully gives the kids a sense of security," Alisha observed. Positive co-parenting also predicted the development of their children's sense of conscience and their ability to make moral decisions.

Reflection Activity

To improve the quality of their relationship and deepen their understanding, Alisha and Rohan engaged in a reflection activity. Each partner reflected on the following questions:

1. What have I received from my partner?

2. What have I given to my partner?

3. What troubles and difficulties have I caused my partner?

They wrote their reflections in a journal and then shared them with each other. This activity promoted gratitude, empathy, and mutual understanding. "Reflecting on our actions and sharing these thoughts helps us appreciate each other more," Rohan noted.

Getting Professional Help

When Alisha and Rohan faced deeper issues, they turned to relationship mediation. This method helped them, as a couple, identify their common commitment to their union and respond flexibly to their issues. A mediator assisted them in opening and improving lines of communication, addressing areas of friction, and developing guidelines for behavioural changes to lessen future conflict. "Mediation has really helped us understand each other better and find ways to move forward constructively," Alisha said.

By implementing these strategies, Alisha and Rohan were able to co-parent effectively, providing a stable and loving environment for their children. Their commitment to communication, understanding, and professional support ensured that their children thrived despite the challenges of co-parenting.

Dialogue:

- Rohan: "Let's use a shared calendar to keep track of the children's activities and appointments."

- Alisha: "Great idea. It will help us stay organized and ensure we're on the same page."

Setting Boundaries: Define clear boundaries regarding parenting roles, responsibilities, and interactions. Respect each other's space and parenting styles, focusing on the best interests of the children.

Dialogue:

- Rohan: "We need to agree on boundaries regarding bedtime routines."

- Alisha: "Yes, let's ensure we have consistent rules in both households."

Conflict Resolution: Address conflicts calmly and constructively. Prioritize finding solutions that benefit the children and avoid involving them in adult disagreements.

Dialogue:

- Alisha: "We have different views on discipline. Can we discuss this and find a middle ground?"

- Rohan: "Absolutely. It's important to find a consistent approach that works for both of us."

Creating a Parenting Plan: Develop a comprehensive parenting plan that outlines custody arrangements, visitation schedules, and decision-making responsibilities. This plan provides a clear framework and reduces uncertainty.

Dialogue:

- Alisha: "Let's create a parenting plan that details our custody arrangements and schedules."

- Rohan: "Agreed. It will help us manage our responsibilities and ensure the children have stability."

Activities and Exercises

Activity: Co-Parenting Workshops:

Attend co-parenting workshops or counselling sessions together. These programs provide valuable tools and techniques for effective co-parenting and offer support from professionals and other co-parents.

Activity:

- Rohan: "I found a co-parenting workshop in our area. Would you be open pen to attending it together?"

- Alisha: "That sounds like a great idea. I'm willing to give it a try."

Example 1: Joint Decision-Making: Practice joint decision

- Alisha: "I have noticed that there have been some deviations from the agreed-upon visitation schedule. Can we discuss how we can make it more consistent?"

- Rohan: "I understand. Let us look at our schedules and see if we can find a solution that works for both of us and ensures consistency for our child."

Example 2: Addressing Communication Breakdowns

- Rohan: "I feel concerned when communication breaks down and important decisions are made without discussion. Can we find a way to improve our communication for the benefit of our child, as well as the benefit of each other?"

- Alisha: "I agree. We can set up regular check-ins to discuss any upcoming events or concerns. This way, we can stay on the same page."

Example 3: Finding Middle Ground on Parenting Styles

- Rohan: "I understand our different parenting styles. Can we work together to find a middle ground that considers both our perspectives for the benefit of our child?"

- Alisha: "Absolutely. Let us list out our parenting priorities and see where we can compromise to create a balanced approach."

- Example 4: Setting Boundaries and Consequences

- Alisha: "It is important for both of us to communicate respectfully. If the conversation becomes disrespectful or unproductive, I may need to step away and revisit this discussion later."

- Rohan: "I understand. Let us agree to take a break if things get heated and come back to the discussion when we're both calm."

Example 5: Discussing Major Life Changes

- Alisha: "I wanted to let you know that I am planning to move to a new apartment next month. How do you think this will affect our co-parenting arrangement?"

- Rohan: "Thanks for letting me know. Let us discuss how the move might impact our child's routine and see if we need to make any adjustments to our schedule."

These examples can help couples navigate co-parenting conversations with empathy and cooperation. For more detailed guidance, you can refer to resources like the Co-Parenting.

Making by discussing and agreeing on important decisions affecting the children, such as education, healthcare, and extracurricular activities.

Example Exercise:

- Rohan: "Let's discuss our options for after-school programs and decide on school programs together."

- Alisha: "I agree. It's important to consider what's best for the children."

Reflective Practice

Self-Reflection and Growth: Engage in regular self-reflection to understand how your actions and decisions impact the co-parenting relationship and your children. Reflect on areas for improvement and celebrate successes.

Example Reflection Prompts:

- How have my actions supported effective co-parenting?

- What challenges have I faced, and how can I address them constructively?

- How can I continue to prioritize the well-being of my children?

Conclusion

Effective co-parenting is essential for providing children with a stable and loving environment. By fostering clear communication, setting boundaries, and addressing conflicts constructively, co-parent parents can work together to support their children's growth and development. Prioritizing the well-being of the children and committing to a collaborative approach ensures that the challenges of co-parenting are met with compassion, respect, and unity.

References

1. Afifi, T. D., & Schrodt, P. (2003). "Feeling Caught" as a Mediator of Adolescents' and Young Adults' Avoidance and Satisfaction with their Parents in Divorced and Nondivorced Households. Communication Monographs,

70(2), 142-173.

2. Amato, P. R., & Gilbreth, J. G. (1999). Nonresident Fathers and Children's Well-Being: A Meta-Analysis. Journal of Marriage and Family, 61(3), 557-573.

3. Kelly, J. B., & Emery, R. E. (2003). Children's Adjustment Following Divorce: Risk and Resilience Perspectives. Family Relations, 52(4), 352-362.

4. McIntosh, J. E., Smyth, B. M., & Kelaher, M. (2010). *Parenting Arrangements Post Separation: Patterns and Developmental Outcomes, Studies of Two Risk Groups

Chapter 5

Co-Parenting Conversations: Navigating Separation with Amiability and Future Friendship

Navigating the waters of co-parenting after separation requires empathy, clear communication, and mutual respect. This chapter explores strategies for separating partners to foster amiable relationships and effective co-parenting. Learn how to set boundaries, maintain open dialogue, and prioritize the well-being of your children. By embracing these practices, couples can transition from partners to co-parents while preserving a foundation of friendship and mutual support.

"Letting go means to come to the realization that some people are a part of your history, but not a part of your destiny." – Steve Maraboli

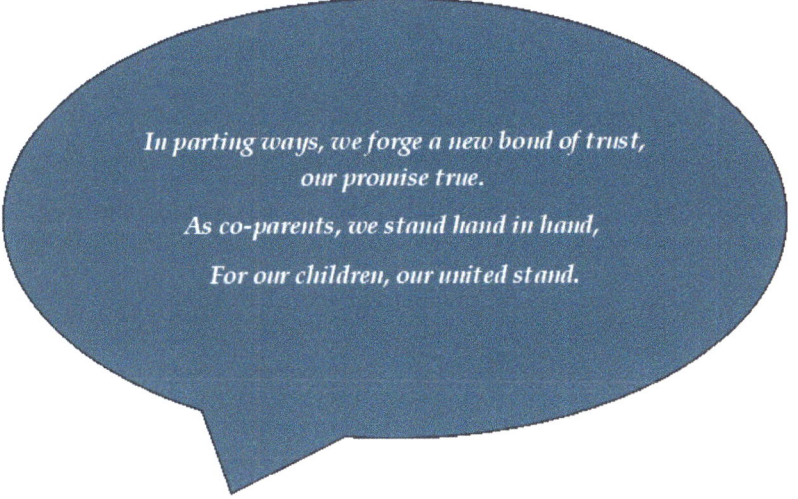

In parting ways, we forge a new bond of trust, our promise true.
As co-parents, we stand hand in hand,
For our children, our united stand.

Ending a romantic relationship is difficult, but when children are involved, it's crucial to approach the separation with a focus on co-parenting. Successful co-parenting requires open communication, respect, and a shared commitment to the

well-being of the children. This chapter offers guidance on how separating partners can navigate these conversations, establish boundaries, and foster a cooperative and supportive co-parenting relationship. Separation can be a challenging and emotional process, but it is possible to part ways amicably and maintain a friendship for the future. This chapter will explore strategies and conversations that can help separating partners achieve this goal.

When Diane and Henry made the tough decision to separate, they knew that thoughtful strategies and open conversations would be essential to achieve a respectful and amicable parting. They decided to choose the right time and place for their initial discussion, selecting a neutral setting where they could talk honestly without distractions. This helped both of them feel comfortable and open to dialogue.

Being honest but tactful was their next step. Diane expressed her feelings and intentions clearly, yet sensitively, avoiding blame and criticism. "I've been feeling distant and think it's best for both of us to move forward separately," she said, ensuring that her honesty was delivered with compassion.

Henry practiced active listening, allowing Diane to express her feelings and concerns without interruption. This showed respect and helped build a foundation for their future friendship. "I hear what you're saying and appreciate you sharing your feelings," Henry responded, making sure Diane felt understood.

As they discussed future arrangements, they tackled practical matters such as finances, property, and child custody. They aimed for mutually agreeable solutions that prioritized the well-being of everyone involved, especially their children. "Let's make sure our decisions are in the best interest of the kids," Henry emphasized.

Recognizing the complexity of their situation, they sought professional assistance from a mediator. The mediator facilitated productive conversations and helped them navigate the intricacies of their separation. "Having a neutral third party really helps us stay focused and constructive," Diane noted.

Establishing clear boundaries was crucial to prevent misunderstandings and give each other space to heal. They set limits on communication and social interactions, understanding that this was necessary for their individual well-being. "We need some space to process everything," Diane acknowledged, setting a foundation for healthy boundaries.

Focusing on the positive aspects of their relationship, Diane and Henry highlighted the good times they shared and expressed gratitude. This helped them move forward with a sense of closure and positivity. "Despite our differences, we had many wonderful moments together," Henry reflected.

Planning for their post-separation relationship, they discussed how they would maintain a friendship. This included regular check-ins, co-parenting arrangements, and social gatherings, all while being realistic about what was feasible and comfortable for both parties. "Let's stay connected in a way that works for both of us," Diane suggested.

To help find closure, Diane and Henry engaged in a reflection activity. They took some time to reflect on the positive memories and lessons learned from their relationship. Diane wrote a letter to Henry, expressing her gratitude and hopes for the future. This exercise helped them both find closure and set the stage for a positive post-separation relationship.

By incorporating these strategies and conversations, Diane and Henry navigated their separation with grace and respect, ensuring a supportive environment for themselves and their children.

Reflection Activity: Take some time to reflect on the positive memories and lessons learned from your relationship. Write a letter to your partner expressing your gratitude and hopes for the future. This exercise can help you find closure and set the stage for a positive post-separation relationship.

"The ultimate test of a relationship is to disagree but to hold hands." - *Alexandra Penney*

Self-Reflection Activity

Activity: Reflecting on Disagreements

1. Think about a recent disagreement you had with your partner. Write down the main points of the disagreement and how it made you feel.

2. Reflect on your response during the disagreement. Did you listen actively? Did you express your feelings clearly and respectfully?

3. Consider your partner's perspective. How do you think they felt during the disagreement? What were their main points?

4. Identify areas for improvement. What could you have done differently to make the conversation more constructive? How can you approach similar situations in the future?

5. Discuss your reflections with your partner. Share your thoughts and listen to their perspective. Use this as an opportunity to strengthen your communication and understanding.

Recognizing the Importance of Amiable Co-Parenting

Child's Well-Being:

Children thrive in environments where parents maintain a respectful and cooperative relationship. Amiable co-parenting reduces stress and provides a sense of stability and security for the children.

Modelling Healthy Relationships:

By working together as co-parents, parents' model healthy conflict resolution, cooperation, and mutual respect. These behaviours are crucial for the emotional and social development of children.

Minimizing Conflict:

Open and respectful communication helps minimize conflict, making it easier to address co-parenting challenges. A collaborative approach ensures that both parents are on the same page and can work together effectively.

Practical Strategies for Co-Parenting Amiably

Establish Clear Boundaries: Define clear boundaries to ensure respect and minimize conflict. This includes setting expectations around communication, parenting responsibilities, and personal space.

Maintain Open Dialogue: Commit to regular, open communication about parenting issues. Use collaborative tools like shared calendars and co-parenting apps to stay organized and aligned.

Dialogue:

- **Diane:** "The shared calendar for our kids' activities needs to be worked according to my shifts as they keep changing fortnightly?"

- **Henry:** "Yes, that's a great idea. It'll help us stay organized and communicate effectively and we could also discuss the progress of our children each week, when we talk about the different schedules."

Focus on the Children: Prioritize the well-being of the children in all decisions. Keep conversations child-centered and avoid involving children in adult conflicts.

Dialogue:

- Henry: "Our 11-year-old has been acting up and refusing to eat nor adhere to the self-care routine. She is sullen and depressed most of the time and I was wondering if you are actually talking to her against me. She has been influencing the other children and they are rebelling against disciplining or rules.

- Diane: "I think the talk is happening in our kids' school and they must have heard me speaking to my parents. I will, however, take this matter on hand and have a chat with them."

Seek Professional Support: Consider seeking the help of a family therapist or mediator to facilitate discussions and resolve conflicts. Professional support can provide valuable tools and strategies for effective co-parenting. Children can be encouraged to attend counselling sessions at school.

Dialogue (after seeking counselling sessions):

- Henry: "I think it has been extremely helpful to have had the kids go to the loss and grief and counselling sessions and also having had you speaking to them. It was imperative that they do not blame themselves nor feel they are to take sides. The counsellor has definitely helped them through this transition."

- Diane: "Professional support has been crucial for us all and I am finding myself too in a better place. Thanks for suggesting and having these open conversations."

Activities and Exercises

Activity: Co-Parenting Agreement: Create a co-parenting agreement that outlines parenting agreement that outlines responsibilities, schedules, and guidelines for decision-making. This document serves as a reference to ensure both parents are aligned.

Example Agreement Sections:

- Parenting schedule and routines

- Decision-making processes

- Communication guidelines

- Dispute resolution methods.

Exercise: Emotional Check-Ins: Schedule regular emotional check-ins to discuss feelings, concerns, and progress. Use this time to address any unresolved issues and celebrate improvements.

Example Check-In Questions:

- How are you feeling about our co-parenting arrangement?

- Are there any challenges we need to address?

- What has been working well in our co-parenting relationship?

Reflective Practice

Self-Reflection and Growth: Engage in regular self-reflection to understand your emotions and how they impact co-parenting. Reflect on what you have learned and how you can apply these insights to foster a healthier co-parenting relationship.

Example Reflection Prompts:

- How have my actions affected our co-parent relationship?

- What steps can I take to improve my communication and cooperation?

- How can I support my co-parent's well-being?

Conclusion

Navigating co-parenting after separation requires empathy, clear communication, and mutual respect. By establishing clear boundaries, maintaining open dialogue, and prioritizing the well-being of the children, separating partners can foster an amiable parenting relationship. This collaborative approach not only benefits the ending relationship. This collaborative approach not only benefits the children but   also promotes personal growth and emotional healing for both parents.

References

1. Hetherington, E. M., & Kelly, J. (2002). For better or for worse: Divorce reconsidered. New York: W.W. Norton & Company.

2. Emery, R. E. (2012). Renegotiating Family Relationships: Divorce, Child Custody, and Mediation. New York: Guilford Press.

3. Beckmeyer, J. J., & Jamison, T. (2016). Co-parenting quality, conflict, and the parenting competence of single mothers and single fathers. Journal of Child and Family Studies, 25(7), 2171-2185.

4. Kelly, J. B., & Emery, R. E. (2003). Children's adjustment following divorce: Risk and resilience perspectives. Family Relations, 52(4), 352-362.

5. McHale, J. P., & Lindahl, K. M. (Eds.).

Chapter 6

New Beginnings: Navigating Remarriage After Divorce

Remarriage after divorce marks a new chapter filled with opportunities for growth and renewed happiness. This chapter explores the unique challenges and joys of entering a new marriage after experiencing a divorce. Learn how to navigate the complexities of blending families, building trust, and fostering a healthy, fulfilling relationship. By approaching remarriage with openness and mutual understanding, couples can create a solid foundation for their new journey together.

"Love can be sweeter the second time around."

In the bloom of second chances,

hearts entwine,

A journey renewed, with love refined.

Through trust and hope, new paths are paved,

A future together, resilient and brave.

Introduction:

Remarrying after a divorce is a testament to resilience and the belief in love's enduring power. It brings with it the promise of new beginnings and the wisdom gained from past experiences. However, it also introduces unique challenges, such as blending families, building trust, and addressing lingering emotional wounds. This chapter delves into the intricacies of navigating remarriage, offering insights and strategies to help couples forge a strong and fulfilling partnership.

Understanding the Challenges of Remarriage

Blending Families: One of the most significant challenges in remarriage is blending families. This involves creating harmonious relationships between stepchildren, managing co-parenting dynamics with ex-spouses, and establishing new family traditions.

Breaking the News to Each Other

Approaching the Conversation: When considering remarriage, it is essential to approach the conversation with sensitivity and openness. Both partners should feel heard

Dialogue:

- Samir: "I've been thinking a lot about our future and feel ready to take the next step in our relationship? How would you like to be the mother of 3 grown-up kids, would you like to get married?

- Shyla: "I've been feeling the same way. Let's discuss what this means for us and our families."

Introducing New Partners

Timing and Sensitivity: Introducing a new partner to children and family members requires careful timing and sensitivity. It is important to ensure that the new relationship is stable and committed before making introductions.

Dialogue:

- Samir to Nerissa: "I'd like to introduce you to someone very special to me. We've been taking things slowly, and I feel it's the right time for you to meet."

- Nerissa: "I'm glad you have found someone to share your life with. I am looking forward to meeting her. Let's plan a comfortable and neutral setting for our introduction."

Dynamics of Blended Families

Children's Perspectives: Children may have mixed emotions about a new partner entering their lives. They might feel excitement, curiosity, or even resentment and confusion. Open communication and reassurance are key to helping children adjust.

Dialogue with Children:

- Parent: "I want to talk to you about someone special in my life. They mean a lot to me, and I hope we can all get to know each other better."

- Child: "I'm not sure how I feel about this."

- Parent: "It's okay to have mixed feelings. Let's take things one step at a time and see how it goes."

Building Relationships: Establishing positive relationships between new partners and children involves patience, understanding, and gradual integration. Activities that foster bonding and mutual respect can ease this transition.

Dialogue:

- Parent: "Let's plan some fun activities together this weekend. It's important for us to spend time as a family."

- Child: "I'd like that. We can go to the park?"

- New Partner: "The park sounds like a great idea. I'm looking forward to spending time with you."

Co-Parenting Dynamics: Navigating co-parenting with an ex-spouse requires clear communication and respectful boundaries. Keeping the child's best interests at the forefront ensures a cooperative and supportive environment.

Dialogue:

- Parent: "I want to discuss how we can co-parent effectively with my new partner involved. Let us make sure we are all on the same page.

- Ex-spouse: "Agreed. It's important for our children to feel supported by all of us."

Dialogue:

- Samir: "We need to think about how we can help our kids adjust to our new family dynamic."

- Nerissa: "Absolutely. Let's involve them in creating new family traditions and ensure they feel valued and included."

Building Trust: Trust is a cornerstone of any relationship, and it can be particularly challenging to rebuild after a divorce. Open communication and consistent actions are essential for fostering trust in a new marriage.

Example Dialogue:

- Nerissa: "I understand that rebuilding trust takes time. Let's commit to being open and honest with each other."

- Samir: "I agree. Trust is built through our everyday actions and communication."

Addressing Emotional Wounds: Both partners may carry emotional baggage from previous relationships. It is important to address these wounds through empathy, patience, and, if necessary, professional support.

Dialogue:

- Samir: "I have some lingering fears from my previous marriage. Can we talk about how we can support each other?"

- Nerissa: "Of course. I want to understand your concerns and work through them together."

Practical Strategies for a Successful Remarriage

Open Communication: Prioritize open and honest communication. Regularly discuss your feelings, expectations, and any concerns that arise. This helps build a foundation of trust and understanding.

Dialogue:

- Nerissa: "How are you feeling about our progress in blending our families?"

- Samir: "I think we're making good strides, but we need to keep communicating openly."

Setting Boundaries: Establish clear boundaries with ex-spouses and other family members. This helps protect the new relationship and ensures that both partners feel secure.

Dialogue:

- Nerissa: "Let's set some boundaries with our ex-spouses to ensure our relationship remains a priority."

- Samir: "I agree. Clear boundaries will help us focus on building our new life together."

Creating New Traditions: Build new family traditions that reflect your combined values and experiences. This fosters a sense of unity and belonging in the new family structure.

Example Dialogue:

- Nerissa: "How about we start a weekly family game night, or a BBQ cook out session?"

- Samir: "Great idea! It will help us bond and create lasting memories and the kids will feel more at home with the new family dynamics."

Activity: Family Meetings: Using old routines where new members are invited to, helps to decrease the uneasiness in both parties. Hold regular family meetings to discuss any issues, plan activities, and share positive experiences. This helps keep communication open and ensures that everyone feels heard.

Example Family Meeting Agenda:

- Discuss any challenges or concerns.

- Plan upcoming family activities.

- Share highlights from the past week.

Activities and Exercises for Blended Families

Activity: Family Meetings: Hold regular family meetings to discuss any issues, plan activities, and share positive experiences. This helps keep communication open and ensures that everyone feels heard.

Example Family Meeting Agenda:

- Discuss any challenges or concerns.

- Plan upcoming family activities.

- Share highlights from the past week.

Exercise: Trust

Building Activities: Engage in activities designed to build trust and strengthen your bond. These can include joint decision-making exercises, trust falls, or even family therapy sessions.

Example Trust-Building Activity:

- **Activity:** Plan a weekend getaway where each partner is responsible for various aspects (e.g., accommodation, activities). This encourages collaboration and trust.

Activity: Creating New Traditions: Establish new family traditions that reflect your combined values and experiences. This fosters a sense of unity and belonging in the new family structure.

189

Self-Reflection and Growth: Reflect on your past experiences and how they shape your current relationship. Consider how you can apply the lessons learned to foster a healthy and fulfilling remarriage.

Example Reflection Prompts:

- What have I learned from my previous marriage that I can apply to my current relationship?

- How can I support my partner in addressing their concerns and fears?

- What steps can we take together to ensure a strong and lasting marriage?

Conclusion

Remarriage after divorce offers a chance for new beginnings and renewed happiness. By addressing the unique challenges with openness, empathy, and mutual support, couples can build a strong and fulfilling partnership. Through open communication, trust-building, and creating new traditions, remarried couples can navigate their new journey with resilience and love.

References

- Ganong, L. H., & Coleman, M. (2004). Stepfamily Relationships: Development, Dynamics, and Interventions. New York: Kluwer Academic/Plenum Publishers.

- Hetherington, E. M., & Kelly, J. (2002). For Better or for Worse: Divorce Reconsidered. New York: W.W. Norton & Company.

- Paper now, P. L. (2013). Surviving and Thriving in Stepfamily Relationships: What Works and What Does Not. New York: Routledge.

- Sweeney, M. M. (2010). Remarriage and Stepfamilies: Strategic Sites for Family Scholarship in the 21st Century. Journal of Marriage and Family, 72(3), 667-684.

- Visher, E. B., & Visher, J. S. (2003). How to Win as a Stepfamily. New York: Routledge.

Chapter 7

The Journey Within: Navigating Life's Challenges with Humanity and Divinity

In the concluding and insightful chapter, we turn inward to explore the spiritual and existential conversations we have with ourselves, our sense of divinity, and our place within humanity and our reasons for our marriage, our relationships, our break ups and achievements. This chapter delves into the essence of navigating life's challenges with a moral compass, seeking support when needed, and striving to be our best selves. Through deliberate and continuous reflections conversations, and harmonious practices, we aim to capture the essence of being human and our best and most honest mirrors are our partners. Through them we learn more about us than anyone else. Facing the truth can sometimes be overwhelming and it is when we begin to understand the true purpose of being called to matrimony or life partnership, we start unravelling a huge mystery of life.

"The privilege of a lifetime is to become who you truly are."— Carl Jung

The more you know yourself, the more clarity there is. Self-knowledge has no end." - Jiddu Krishnamurti

In whispers of the soul, we find our way,

through shadows and light, we face each day.
With hearts as compass and spirits aligned,

In our humanness, the divine we find.

Introduction:

Life's journey is replete with challenges, reflections, and moments of profound insight. As we navigate this path, our inner dialogue with ourselves, our sense of our innate spirituality and our connection to other human beings especially our family at close quarters, they can become our guiding forces. This chapter seeks to encapsulate the essence of the entire book and how we can through meaningful and purpose-filled conversations, reflect deeply and strive for harmony in our lives.

As we explore and continue to access relationships in our life, one is usually guided by how to maintain a moral compass, seek help and support during overwhelming times, and embrace our full humanity while acknowledging the divine spark within us. By doing so, we honor our journey and the profound connections that shape our existence.

We will also explore the importance of connecting with our inner divine self. This connection is essential for personal growth and maintaining a healthy relationship with our partner. By understanding and reconciling with our inner divine self, we can achieve a deeper sense of peace and harmony in our lives.

Engaging in Inner Dialogue

Conversations with your Spouse in your soul-searching journey:

Engaging in honest and compassionate conversations with oneself is foundational for personal growth. This involves acknowledging our fears, aspirations, and values, and understanding our true nature.

Example Reflection:

- Dwi: "What are your deepest fears Sandra, and how can you confront them with courage?"

- Sandra: "What brings me anxious moment and how can I take control of that. I do wish I never have to be alone dear."

Connecting with Divinity:

Whether through prayer, meditation, or quiet contemplation, connecting with a sense of divinity helps us find meaning and purpose. It allows us to transcend our immediate concerns and align with a higher purpose.

Example Reflection:

- Dwi: "Perhaps you can feel the presence of the divine as we have learnt in our Marriage Encounter program, remember, we were asked to take everything to God. Find out what he has planned for us and that way, you do not need to worry."

- Sandra: "You are so right Dwi, in doing do I feel lighter, I can serve others and bring light into the world?"

Navigating Life's Challenges

Maintaining a Moral Compass: Our moral compass guides us through ethical dilemmas and tough decisions. Reflecting on our values and principles ensures that we act with integrity and kindness.

Reflection:

- Dwi: "Am I living in alignment with my core values?"

- Sandra: "Reflect on the choices you make daily and know whether you have peace at the end of it or turmoil dear Dwi, what do you think?

- Dwi: "you are so right Sandra, when our choices are in alignment with our values, we will be at peace.". Thank you Sandra."

Seeking Help and Support:

Recognizing when we need help and reaching out for support is a sign of strength, not weakness. Building a network of trusted individuals and resources provides the support we need during challenging times.

Dialogue:

- Patrick: "I'm feeling overwhelmed. Who can I turn to for support and guidance?"

- Christina: "Honey, think how you can prioritize self-care to better navigate this challenging period and things that are urgent and important as well?"

Striving to Be Our Best Selves: Constantly striving for personal growth involves embracing our imperfections and learning from our experiences. This journey of self-improvement is both human and divine.

Reflection:

- Jaimini "What lessons have I learned from my struggles, and how can I apply them moving forward?"

- Nita: "Basically Jai, I think whenever you have had struggles and have overcome them, it has made you more compassionate and understanding in your interactions with others, has it not?"

- Jaimini: "Indeed Nita it has, thanks for throwing light on that aspect."

Reflections and Harmonious Practices

Journaling: Maintain a journal to document your thoughts, reflections, and spiritual experiences. Writing provides clarity and helps track your growth and insights over time.

Journal Entry:

- Self: "Today, I reflected on my core values and realized the importance of what is my true authenticity in my life."

Activity: Meditation

Meditation is a powerful tool for connecting with your inner divine self. Try the following meditation exercise:

1. Find a quiet, comfortable space where you will not be disturbed.

2. Sit or lie down in a relaxed position.

3. Close your eyes and take a few deep breaths, focusing on your breath as it enters and leaves your body.

4. Visualize a warm, glowing light at the center of your being. This light represents your inner divine self.

5. As you continue to breathe deeply, imagine this light growing brighter and expanding throughout your body.

6. Spend a few minutes basking in the warmth and light of your inner divine self.

7. When you are ready, slowly open your eyes and take a moment to reflect on your experience.

Reflection

After completing the meditation exercise, take some time to journal about your experience. Consider the following prompts:

- How did it feel to connect with your inner divine self?

- What insights or revelations did you gain during the meditation?

- How can you incorporate this practice into your daily routine?

Meditation and Mindfulness: Incorporate meditation and mindfulness practices into your daily routine. These practices foster inner peace, self-awareness, and a deeper connection to the present moment.

Meditation Prompt:

- Self: "Focus on your breath and let go of any tension. Reflect on a moment of gratitude and allow it to fill your heart."

Connecting with Nature: Spending time in nature can be a profound spiritual practice. It reminds us of our interconnectedness with the world and provides a space for reflection and renewal.

Reflection:

- Self: "How does nature reflect the beauty and complexity of my own inner world?"

- Self: "In what ways can I honor and protect the natural world around me?"

- **Reflective Practice**

Self-Reflection and Growth: Engage in regular self-reflection to understand your emotions and how they impact the relationship. Reflect on what you have learned and how you can apply these insights to foster a healthier connection.

Example Reflection Prompts:

- Self: "How have I contributed to the emotional dilemmas in our relationship?" "What steps can I take to improve my communication and empathy?" "How can I support my partner's emotional well-being and in doing so, become the best version of myself?" For is it not that we grow when we learn to serve and be a giver?".

Conclusion

Connecting with your inner divine self is a lifelong journey that requires patience, dedication, and self-compassion. By nurturing this connection, you can cultivate a deeper sense of inner peace and harmony, which will positively impact your relationship with your partner.

Navigating life's challenges with humanity and divinity involves engaging in meaningful inner dialogues, maintaining a moral compass, seeking support, and striving for continuous growth. Counselling and psychotherapy help in the journey of self-reflection and enhance our abilities to become aware of our shadow selves and how we can embrace our full humanity and acknowledge the spirituality and our divine self. We find harmony and purpose in our journey of self-growth and knowledge. As we move towards self-learning, we bring to life self-actualization and spiritual fulfilment. We hope you have gained enlightenment, harmony and love from your leadership and indulged in the activities and self-reflections.

References

- Jung, C. G. (1961). Memories, Dreams, Reflections. New York: Vintage.

- Frankl, V. E. (1959). Man's Search for Meaning. Boston: Beacon Press.

- Kabat-Zinn, J. (1994). Wherever You Go, There You Are: Mindfulness Meditation in Everyday Life. New York: Hyperion.

- Neff, K. (2011). Self-Compassion: The Proven Power of Being Kind to Yourself. New York: HarperCollins.

- Tolle, E. (2004). The Power of Now: A Guide to Spiritual Enlightenment. Novato, CA: New World Library.

Acknowledgments

With heartfelt gratitude, I acknowledge God, my faith and the Holy Spirit for continuously guiding and reminding me of my dream. This divine guidance has been my unwavering beacon of light, illuminating my path every step of the way.

To my beloved parents, thank you for always believing in my abilities and providing me with the foundation to pursue my passions. Your love and encouragement have been instrumental in shaping who I am today.

My deepest appreciation goes to my wonderful husband, Brendon Monteiro, for being my steadfast supporter throughout this journey. Your unwavering belief in me and our shared dreams have made this accomplishment possible. Your love and dedication have been my rock.

To my amazing children, who exemplify commitment to their marriages with such dedication and love, I am immensely proud of you. Your relationships are a testament to the values we cherish.

A special thank you to the Marriage Encounter movement, my teachers, and mentors who have played a pivotal role in shaping my understanding of relationships and personal growth. Your wisdom and guidance have been invaluable, and I am deeply grateful.

Lastly, I extend my heartfelt appreciation to all those who have supported me, whether through encouragement, advice, or simply being there. Each of you has contributed to this journey, and I am profoundly thankful.

www.ingramcontent.com/pod-product-compliance
Lightning Source LLC
Chambersburg PA
CBHW051516120626
46551CB00012B/945